MIGHT AS WELL LAUGH
ABOUT IT NOW

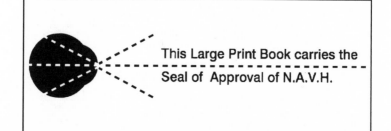

This Large Print Book carries the
Seal of Approval of N.A.V.H.

MIGHT AS WELL LAUGH ABOUT IT NOW

MARIE OSMOND WITH MARCIA WILKIE

THORNDIKE PRESS
A part of Gale, Cengage Learning

GALE
CENGAGE Learning

Detroit • New York • San Francisco • New Haven, Conn • Waterville, Maine • London

GALE
CENGAGE Learning‍

Copyright © Marie, Inc. 2009.
Thorndike Press, a part of Gale, Cengage Learning.

Thorndike Press® Large Print Biography.
The text of this Large Print edition is unabridged.
Other aspects of the book may vary from the original edition.
Set in 16 pt. Plantin.
Printed on permanent paper.

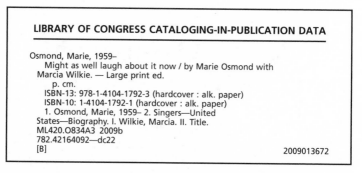

LIBRARY OF CONGRESS CATALOGING-IN-PUBLICATION DATA

Osmond, Marie, 1959–
    Might as well laugh about it now / by Marie Osmond with Marcia Wilkie. — Large print ed.
        p. cm.
    ISBN-13: 978-1-4104-1792-3 (hardcover : alk. paper)
    ISBN-10: 1-4104-1792-1 (hardcover : alk. paper)
    1. Osmond, Marie, 1959– 2. Singers—United States—Biography. I. Wilkie, Marcia. II. Title.
ML420.O834A3 2009b
782.42164092—dc22
    [B]   2009013672

Published in 2009 by arrangement with NAL Signet, a member of Penguin Group (USA) Inc.

Printed in the United States of America
1 2 3 4 5 6 7 13 12 11 10 09

I'm often asked if I had stage parents.

I answer, "Absolutely! They were there for me every *stage* of my life."

To my mother and father, Olive and George Osmond.

In their wisdom they chose to laugh every single day. Now, every single day, I choose to do the same.

My mom and dad celebrating my Roy Acuff award with me.

Osmond Family Archive

CONTENTS

7

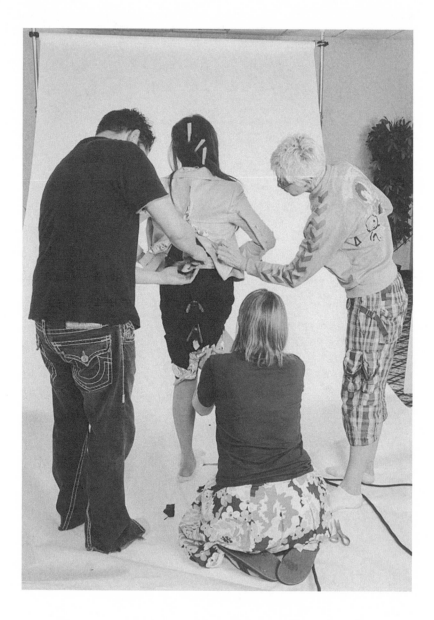

I've never regretted following my intuition. Sometimes it has to shout to be heard over the noise of my crazy and hectic life, but sooner or later I do listen. If I'm wise and want to save myself a lot of unneeded stress, it's sooner.

Has my intuition made my life more fulfilling or even easier? In the long run, yes. In the immediate future, the answer most likely is no. The direction I get from my intuition usually involves either a big leap of faith or, at the very least, a hassle. This book is the result of a small hassle, a huge hassle, then a big leap of faith, which brought me the immense gift of recounting my many blessings and the valuable life lessons that keep me moving forward every day.

Labor Day weekend of 2005, I had a speaking engagement for a group of young women at a retreat outside of Los Angeles. I often take advantage of these quick work trips as a chance to take along one of my kids for some solo Mommy time. This trip my daughter Brianna, who was then seven, would have me all to herself. We planned to fly into Burbank and stay at "Aunt" Patty's house (my best friend since age ten, Patty Leoni). Patty has no children of her own, so I've told her that she needs to help me raise all of mine! My kids love her as much as I do.

As I was packing, my intuition nudged me with the thought that I should take my youngest daughter, Abby, on this trip as well. Of course, I dismissed it. Abby was two and a half at that time and already had a very big personality. She enjoys life in a huge way. On the other hand, when she's stubborn, she's a small mountain. It would have been too much to handle a rambunctious toddler. Besides, she was in the process of potty training, and that alone takes a watchful eye.

I checked in on Brianna to make sure she was packing a swimsuit so she could go in Aunt Patty's pool. I looked over at Abby, napping in her crib. Again, my intuitive voice said: "Take her, too."

"No," I thought, "it's not practical. Abby doesn't know how to swim and it will be too dangerous around Patty's pool." Besides, Patty has gorgeous décor and many delicate collectibles that I was certain Abby would not be able to resist getting her pudgy little fingers on. No. I wouldn't take her this trip.

I picked out something to wear the next day for the speech. As I was zipping up the garment bag, my intuition informed me that, like it or not, I really needed to take Abby along.

"Okay," I thought. "Fine! I give in. I don't know why I'm taking Abby, but I will."

I had to double-time it to get the packing done. As I located all of the gear a toddler needs for a two-day trip, my logical side was berating my decision. My list was long and my time was short and so was my patience. I had about five minutes to pack clothing, diapers, baby wipes, sippy cups, binkies, blankies, a swim vest, a car seat, toys, baby sunblock, and a stroller before I needed to leave for the airport. This fun mommy-daughter trip was suddenly a lot more complicated, going from two small carry-on bags to four checked bags.

My thoughts were still the same the next morning as I stood at Patty's bathroom mirror, trying to put on makeup and focus on my speech while Abby stood at my knees

13

practicing her own favorite new phrase: "Why, Mommy?"

I would soon be able to answer that question for myself. As Patty and I loaded the little girls into her car to head out to the mountains for my engagement, my cell phone rang.

A good friend of mine was calling to tell me that my house was on fire and it was being shown on the morning news. The fire had started in the garage. The gas tanks of two WaveRunners we stored there had caused a huge explosion and the fire had spread very rapidly.

The first words out of my mouth were, "Where are my kids?"

My friend reassured me that all of my children were safe from harm. My home office and Abby and Brianna's shared bedroom were on the side of the house that was consumed in flames. The good news was that the fire department was quickly on the scene, preventing the entire house from going up in a blaze.

My first reaction was tears of relief. Somehow I knew, listening to my friend, that it was going to be okay in the big picture. I turned to look at my two little girls riding in the back of the car. Abby, not understanding this news development, sat in her car seat, chatting to the doll Aunt Patty had given her. I was overwhelmed with gratitude that my children were all safe, and filled with awe as I understood why my intuition had told me to take Abby along on this trip. What if she had been in her crib? Even if she wasn't, I knew my curious and strong-willed baby could have been in great danger. I shuddered to think of the ramifications if she had been there.

It wasn't until I returned home that I realized the extent of the loss. My home office was nonexistent: almost everything was either melted or burned up altogether.

Among my possessions in the completely destroyed category were my personal journals that I had started writing, at my mother's urging, at age ten. Over thirty years of memories of places I've traveled, people I've worked with, career highlights, struggles in love and life, great times with family, becoming a mother to each of my children, cute moments from the kids, funny stuff that happened along the way, the hard times, and much more were gone.

After the insurance company estimated the damage I remarked to a friend, "Maybe we shouldn't rebuild it. We could just put the house on the market with some truthful advertising: 'Large, open floor plan. Lots of natural light. Great mountain views.' "

She added, "Don't forget 'drive-thru kitchen.' "

Dealing with the many repercussions of the fire kept me from giving the journals much thought at all, except the notion that it was probably a blessing in disguise because I'm certain I would have been embarrassed to have my children . . . or anyone . . . read my free-form, four a.m., dyslexic, often unintelligible musings.

About a year after the fire, my manager called to say that several publishing houses were interested in having me write my full autobiography. I responded: "What? Come on! I'm only half dead!"

I wasn't ready to do that kind of public retrospective, but when I thought it over in a more personal way, I realized how much some of my experiences and their resulting insights had helped to shape my outlook on life. Perhaps someday those perceptions would be of interest to my children, just as I'm fascinated reading my own mother's journals now. I asked Marcia Wilkie, the coauthor of my first book, *Behind the Smile,* to help me write down some of my memories.

We found ourselves laughing, crying, and seeing the now-deeper significance of each incident and adventure, even if it was not understood at the time I was going through it. Marcia then suggested that the stories reflected common experiences shared by many others, and that they might benefit people beyond my immediate family.

Growing up in the entertainment business, I have lived much of my life in the public eye. Many of these stories are very personal so it felt like a big leap of faith to make them public, but then I looked at it from a different point of view. I had gained so much insight over the years from people who shared their personal experiences with me, from something as simple as how to amuse a child with a colander to something as profound as how to survive incredible loss. I saw a common trait in those who moved forward through life with admirable enthusiasm — each of them believed that the best way to face hardship is with a good sense of perspective and an even better sense of humor. From the time I was a small girl I began to live by the thought that if you're going to laugh about it in the future, well . . . you might as well laugh about it now!

Written here are my thoughts on some of my life experiences, thoughts inherited from a bevy of wise women . . . and even some men!! We decided to write them in short "busy-person-friendly" chapters, as stand-alone essays rather than a chronological narrative.

I'm blessed with good friends and countless living angels in my life, so I've decided to identify others only by what they do for a living or as a "friend." I would never want anyone to feel left out or overlooked. After all, this book represents only a small handful of the numerous ways my life has been changed by others. Only public figures, my family members, my best friend, Patty, and my longtime manager and guardian angel, Karl, will be written about by name.

I've been as accurate on the who, where, and when as my memory — and maybe my brothers' memories — will allow. Intuition works well for me in the present moment, but it's not so great for recalling the past. Growing up as I did in a performing family, my memories of the hundreds of places we have been and the thousands of people we have met sometimes blend together. Besides, with a family as big as mine, the "who" is often impossible to keep track of. Eight brothers, eight kids, numerous nieces, nephews, and now grandnieces and grandnephews arriving at every turn — my memory bank is full!!

I can't promise that I've remembered events in the order in which they occurred, but this book isn't about looking back. It's a collection of thoughts that have kept me moving forward. I hope you will feel the appreciation I have for my many blessings, including you! Please feel free to laugh at my wonderful, crazy, and challenging life. I do.

— Marie Osmond

THE MOST UNFORGETTABLE MOMENT I'LL NEVER REMEMBER

We came up with a spoof of Dancing with the Stars *for YouTube called "Dancing with the Starved"! This is filmmaker Liz Lachman, writer Marcia Wilkie, dance partner Jonathan Roberts and me as my doll and me as me . . . getting down with some fun.*
Osmond Family Archive

Jane Seymour is a doll. The other women on season five of *Dancing with the Stars* were also dolls, but there was no question that Jane was the biggest doll. Though I was the "original" doll among the five remaining female celebrity competitors on the show, all of us could claim immortality in vinyl.

We had all been modeled into twelve-inch Barbie-style play dolls at some point in our careers. My play doll debuted during the original *Donny and Marie* variety show, when I was sixteen years old. Mel B had her look-alike Spice Girl doll. Jennie Garth had been made into a Kelly Taylor doll, her character from *Beverly Hills, 90210.* Sabrina Bryan was the most current doll as Dorinda of the Cheetah Girls. Jane Seymour's *Dr. Quinn, Medicine Woman* doll was made of porcelain, elegantly costumed, and towered two inches over our dolls, making her the biggest doll.

Being dolls might never have come up in conversation among the five of us, except that I made a video spoof about rehearsing for *Dancing with the Stars* featuring my Marie doll.

I decided to make the video, "Dancing with the Starved," because I had to find a way to laugh about the situation I had put myself in. I was on a ballroom dancing show and I didn't know how to dance! My brothers and I had learned some basic tap steps growing up, but most of our dance moves were very similar to *Saturday Night Fever* steps: a lot of pointing, a few lunges, big scoops with the arms, and constant head bobbing.

Heading into the first week of rehearsals with my professional partner, Jonathan Roberts, I had no illusions that I'd be a "natural" at the technique of ballroom. I knew it would take a lot of effort. I did, however, fool myself into thinking that I was in pretty good shape. I had lost some weight with NutriSystem and had been walking, as well as doing some yoga, biking, and hiking. I thought I was somewhat prepared for the road ahead. Think again! After the first three hours, I was more like roadkill! There are moves involved in ballroom dancing that require so much flexibility, I didn't know how any person with an actual skeleton could possibly do them.

After my second day of rehearsals, my muscles were so sore I had to crawl up the stairs to my bedroom. I thought if I could lie down for fifteen or twenty minutes I would no longer "feel the burn" in *every* single connective tissue in my body and would soon be fine again. I should have known better. The moment I stopped moving, my body tried to hang up the "Closed for the Season" sign. I could barely pop the childproof cap off of the bottle of ibuprofen. The thought of getting up for a glass of water was unbearable, so I called out to the first kid who passed by the bedroom door. It was my ten-year-old, Brandon.

"Sweetheart, can you get Mommy a glass of water?"

"I can't carry anything else right now, Mom," he told me, displaying his full hands to me.

By this time, I couldn't really turn my neck to see what he was preoccupied with.

"Just set that stuff here on the bed and run quick and get me a glass of water. Okay?"

Brandon shrugged. "Okay. I guess. Don't squash it."

He unloaded his hands onto the bed and

disappeared out the door.

In my peripheral vision, I could see that the object that Brandon was worried about me squashing was now moving toward me. It only took a second to register that it was his pet snake, Hisssssss.

When Brandon had acquired the snake two months earlier, I had told him he could keep it in an aquarium in his room with the understanding that I didn't want to have to feed it, touch it, hear it, clean it, or even see it if at all possible. I like pets with four feet and a neck, not pets that are four feet long and can wrap around your neck! If it can't wear a collar, I'd rather it lived with someone else. I've always liked pets that can greet you at the door — not ones that slither across your pillow when you're helplessly immobile with muscles that have locked up. A week before, I would have jumped up and run into the bathroom, slamming the door behind me, until the snake was taken away, but all I could do was lay there in pain, watching Hissssss stick his tongue out at me.

I thought about Eve in the Garden of Eden, being "chatted up" by the serpent. I like to think that if I were Eve, I would never have fallen for a delicious forbidden apple and my perfect life of simplicity in the garden would have gone on and on and on. Probably the only irritation Eve faced pre-serpent was Adam complaining that his abs would never look great because he was missing a rib.

But, lying on my bed in pain, I was seeing it all from a different perspective. I would have traded paradise for a massage, a bath full of Epsom salts, and that glass of water so I could take this ibuprofen.

So I could be at home with my children as much as possible, Jonathan commuted to Utah every Wednesday through Saturday to teach me the dance or multiple dances we would be performing the following Monday on live television for 22 to 25 million viewers. Some teachers give you only information. Others, like Jonathan, give you skills and confidence to be the best possible. He was a perfect teacher and guide for me.

After the kids went off to school in the morning, I met with a physical trainer for an hour to help me through stretching exercises so I could be limber enough to rehearse with Jonathan. Then Jonathan and I started the process of learning the new dances. Bit by bit, we rehearsed every move again and again, for at least four hours. The show's camera crew was at almost every rehearsal and seemed thrilled to catch any slip, stumble, sweaty brow, look of frustration, and inability to pull off a move. I'm pretty sure they had an endless supply from my rehearsals alone.

After rehearsal, I'd race out the door (or limp out, to be more exact) to be home when the kids arrived, have dinner with them, and squeeze in some family time. Usually around nine p.m., when the younger ones were all in bed, I'd change back into dance clothes and meet with Jonathan again from ten p.m. to one a.m. As soon as my aching body would adjust to one set of dance moves, it would be time to move on to a whole new ballroom style and even more complicated choreography.

On Sunday, Monday, and Tuesday, we rehearsed on the set during the day, did the shows, and then rehearsed for the next week every night. I had to make room in my memory bank for hundreds of new dance steps, so I erased my brothers' names and their birthdays. Sorry, Tito, Marlon, and Jermaine.

The costume fittings happened on Sunday mornings and then it was off to the spray-tan room. If I hadn't been self-conscious enough about the revealing costumes and having four sets of wardrobe assistants' hands push and pull my body into spandex and fishnets and corsets and push-ups and squish-downs . . . well, the spray-tan room would finish the job, quick.

The first time I went in the spray-tan room the assistant smiled at me and said: "Strip!"

"Excuse me?"

"Completely naked," she said, not even looking up from her paperwork.

"Where's the tanning booth?" I asked, looking around the room.

"No booth," she replied. "Just me and this."

She held up a can the size of a fire extinguisher sporting a hose with a gun-shaped nozzle on the end.

She wasn't one to mince words, and since it was season five, she was probably used to people being shocked the first time. (By week ten, it seemed as casual as taking your car into a drive-through car wash.)

"Just kill me now," I said with a reluctant grin and started to undress. "So much for modesty."

Fifteen minutes later I looked like a construction cone.

"This may not be my color," I tried to suggest.

"It's perfect," she confirmed. "It never looks good in real life, but on TV you'll look great. Be careful, though. It can rub off."

That was her only understatement.

I stayed at my friend Patty's house for all of the Los Angeles rehearsals and show dates because I felt so much more at home there than in a hotel. I could also take turns bringing one or two of the kids in with me every week to see "Aunt Patty."

Over the first few weeks I unintentionally turned many of her sheets, pillowcases, and towels a bright orange. The insides and collars of all my clothing had turned orange, as had the handles of my purse, my car's steering wheel, and any book I touched. It was as if I had emerged from a bag of Cheetos.

After the third week, Patty wised up and gave me my very own set of "already ruined" sheets and towels.

"I've gone through three bottles of bleach in two weeks," Patty told me in her fake scolding manner. "Here are your pillowcases. They used to be white. Now they look like tie-dye. Don't touch the walls. Don't sit on the good couch!"

Every Tuesday, one celebrity was eliminated from the show. I suggested they change that term to "exfoliated" so that no one would have to leave with horrible bright orange skin.

Heading into the competition, I knew there would be a few obstacles that I'd have to conquer, like learning the dances and getting in shape, and a few obstacles that I could do nothing about. The biggest obstacle? Ballroom dancing, by its form, naturally shows off the flair and skills of the female partner. Though the males, of course, play an important part, they rarely do spins, leg lifts, splits, or anything that requires being upside down! When you watch ballroom dancing, it's almost impossible to not watch the woman. The women celebrities on the show, in essence, had to compete against the professional female dancers. Not an easy task. The female professional dancers on that show were all phenomenal! The other reality that I could do nothing about was the lineup of celebrities. Most of them were ten to twenty years younger than me.

In fact, Jane Seymour, Wayne Newton, and I were the only three who were alive when man first walked on the moon.

I decided to have a blast despite the odds. I told the press that I was doing the show for all the people in midlife who felt that their lives were over. I wanted to prove that we don't have to stop trying new challenges just because we've crossed the 4-0 bridge.

I started to joke around backstage with the other dancers and everyone on the staff and crew. With Jane Seymour on hand to represent the "dignified" woman so elegantly, I felt that I could be the "goof" that I truly am.

Jane and I shared the same extra-long dressing room trailer on the lot. It was divided in the middle into two separate and private spaces. Jane's half was beautifully arranged with fresh flowers and art. Classical music and the scent of essential oils wafted from her door as she entered and exited. My half was more like your average Chuck E. Cheese pizzeria on a Saturday afternoon. Piled in one corner were toys, coloring books, and markers. On the shelves were video-game players, laptops, printers, and boxes of promo photos. The floor had dog bowls and chew sticks. Packages of Nu-triSystem crammed the closet shelf and the countertops were strewn with bags of red licorice (low-fat candy), show jewelry, tubes of muscle rub, and boxes of bandages for my blisters. If you opened the door to my side of the trailer too quickly, a stack of Marie Osmond doll boxes would topple out to the walkway. I had passed around my doll catalogue and told the staff and crew that they could order my dolls "at cost" if they were interested. I had no idea it would come to about eighty dolls!! After the first couple of weeks, a trailer that had emptied out was filled with doll boxes and became a satellite distribution center.

I knew that the producers loved it to look like the celebrities were in a fierce competition with each other, but the way I saw it was: Who needed stress on top of physical pain? Besides, it was a really fun group of people.

When the twenty-two-year-old Sabrina Bryan got perfect "10s" from the judges in one of the early weeks, someone backstage asked Wayne Newton if he thought he'd ever get a ten as a score. He chuckled and said: "I already did. I got two fives."

As Tom Bergeron, the host, prepares to go to commercial break, the camera pans the backstage "holding room," and all the dancers usually smile and wave to the camera. The first week I held up a banana peel, as if I were going to use it as a weapon to wipe out the competition. That seemed to get the other couples loosened up and pretty soon everyone was playing out little scenarios before the commercial breaks.

I started to get e-mails from younger viewers telling me that I was fun to watch, and comments from many others saying that it was great that I wasn't taking myself so seriously, as others on previous seasons had done. Hearing this feedback led me to the idea of doing the YouTube sketch. I've never had a problem making fun of myself, my background, or my career.

In the first YouTube sketch I did a voice-over for my doll, which was "rehearsing" for *Dancing with the Stars.* We taped it in a little gym above an apartment complex on the west side of Los Angeles. I used my chipper 1970s voice, until I made a real appearance toward the end of the sketch with Jonathan. He was completely willing to be as goofy as me, and I'll always love him for that.

The video got so many hits on YouTube that *Entertainment Tonight* got their hands on a copy and ran with it for the closing minute of one of their shows. The other celebrities saw how much fun we had making the original and were eager to get on board. Once we realized that all the female celebrities had dolls in their likeness, the idea for a YouTube catfight bloomed ("Girls Night Ouch").

Each of the women contributed voice-overs for their dolls and then made a cameo appearance in the end, after the surprise twist with *All My Children* soap star Cameron Mathison, who jumped in to play along. Cameron is as sweet and authentic as the guy next door. (The really, really, really good-looking guy next door.) Both of the videos still play on YouTube.com. Take a look.

As many hits as each of those videos received on YouTube, my most-watched video, a million times over, was the one of me falling to the floor, unconscious. Talk about doing something unexpected before a commercial break!

When I stepped out on the dance floor with Jonathan for that samba, I already felt light-headed. Less than twenty miles from the television studios, the hills of Malibu, California, were on fire. A brush fire had caught hold and acre after acre of land, along with some homes, were burning out of control. The air over Los Angeles was full of ash and the smell of burning wood. I had been coughing much of the day from the bad air quality. Now, posing for the opening moment of our dance, I was feeling sluggish and exhausted. As the band began, I wasn't able to keep up with Jonathan the way I had earlier in rehearsal. I was missing simple moves that we had practiced a thousand times. The audience became a complete blur and the music sounded warped in my ear.

Somehow, I got through it. However, when we walked over to the judges' table to get our critique, I could tell that I was fading out quickly. I've fainted a couple of times before, from a combination of allergies and stress, so I could recognize the warning signals that preceded fainting.

Tom Bergeron looked at me like I was a crazy woman when I started jumping up and down while Bruno was talking to me, but I was desperately trying to shake off the feeling of fainting. It didn't help. As soon as I stood still to listen to Len Goodman's critique, a black veil closed off my vision and down I went.

The director went to a long commercial break, leaving millions of viewers to wonder if I had "flown the coop."

When I came to, I looked up into my son Stephen's face. He and my daughter Rachael had been sitting in the front row of the audience with my brother Jay and my manager, Karl. Stephen was holding my head and Jay had my hand in his. I didn't realize where I was until Tom Bergeron's face loomed over me and Jonathan came into view. Then I said, "Oh, crap!" because I knew that I had "decked it" on national television.

After a couple of minutes, I was fine to

walk and wanted to make sure the studio audience knew that I was okay, so I decided to take a bow, as if the faint were a "death drop" at the end of my samba. I didn't want anyone to worry; I knew that, though it was embarrassing, I would soon be fine.

The show executives had called in paramedics, who ran a few tests and concluded that it was a simple fainting spell and the only thing they could do for the knot that had sprouted on my head was an ice pack or two. The other celebrities and professional dancers were very sweet, rushing every food and drink imaginable to my side to improve my blood sugar. For the rest of the show, the producers insisted that I lie on a couch in one of the guest star dressing rooms.

By the second hour of the show, eastern time, the middle of the country was seeing the first hour. Karl was being inundated with calls from family and friends who had just watched me pass out on live television and had no idea what had occurred.

As my close friends and family gathered around me in the dressing room, the impact of my fainting on television began to sink in. I felt horrible about scaring so many people and shutting down the production for even five minutes.

One of the show producers came into the room to check on me.

"I'm so sorry," I apologized to him.

"We want to make sure you're absolutely okay," he told me, "but, please, don't feel bad for the sake of the show. That was the most dramatic moment on television all season!"

A full spectrum of reactions to my fainting followed in the days to come. Some people thought that I'd done it as a joke. Others thought it was terrifying. Comments flew around on the Internet that I had faked the faint to raise my scores. All I can say is, try faking a faint and hitting the floor with that amount of force sometime! The thud that could be heard when I landed was definitely not a sound effect.

I received thousands of e-mails of encouragement and support. Many people wrote to me that my willingness to get back on my feet and back into the competition inspired them to take chances and reach for their own goals. For the remaining weeks of the show, even on those rehearsal days when I thought I couldn't go on, I did it for my fans. I couldn't stand the thought of letting them down.

As much as it would have been great to be remembered for improving as a dancer from the first week to the last, I know that my most memorable appearance on *Dancing with the Stars* will always be those two minutes that I was completely unconscious.

Larry King said to me during an interview on his show a year later: "Look how it boosted your career. Even though many people know you didn't win, if people think of that *Dancing with the Stars*, you're the winner."

It seems that even our most embarrassing moments can come with their share of gifts. Maybe Eve had an insight in choosing the apple, for which she rarely receives credit.

Perhaps she knew that we would appreciate our opportunities more if we put the effort into making the best of them. If she and Adam had stayed put in the garden they might have remained oblivious to pain and sorrow, but they would have never experienced what effort brings with it: a sense of accomplishment and great joy.

By the way, the winner of the coveted disco ball that season was the champion race car driver Helio Castroneves. Sure, he was charming with Julianne Hough, but I thought Mel B should have won. She did a series of three full moving splits in her final Viennese Waltz. Come on!!! Let's see Helio do even one!

BE STILL

After traveling with eight brothers in Japan, I think this was a mood swing!
Osmond Family Archive

This was how I asked for directions when I was living in Utah: "Just tell me, do I drive toward the mountains or away from them?" Huge landmarks are the only way I can get my bearings. Street names, intersections, sections of town, or any mention of longitude or latitude is like a foreign language to me. I'm certain it's from spending so much of my life on the road, changing locations every two or three days to a new city, state, or even country. Figuring out how to get from point A to point B seems better left to the landmarks and the locals.

My oldest daughter, Jessica, gave me a GPS system for my car.

"I saw it in the window of an electronics store," she told me. "I knew it would rock your world. It talks to you. Tells you exactly where to go. All you have to do is listen."

She paused for a moment, and then said, "That might be the difficult part for you."

Jessica has always been my practical child. I don't think she's ever bought anything that she hasn't used over and over again. She does not know the meaning of buyer's remorse. I admire that, especially since my charge-card statements often have as many credits from returns as they have purchases. It's funny how those things you "can't live without" become things you "can't live with" once you get them home. Melon-colored Lucite high heels, anyone?

I made a valid attempt to have the GPS become my traveling companion, with its authoritative female voice giving commands on how to drive. Perhaps it's from growing up with seven older brothers, but I don't like being bossed around.

The audio direction might be something like "turn right in 350 feet." Math was never my strong suit, so I would try to visualize how far 350 feet is in my head. Is that a football field? Football fields always seem longer to me, and before the voice can say "turn here" I'm already a block past it. If I heard my GPS chick say "recalculating" one more time, I was going to recalculate her right out of my car window!

I live in Las Vegas now, and one of the many bonuses is that I can see the Strato-sphere and the taller attractions on the Strip from anywhere in town. It's also pretty handy that our show at the Flamingo Hotel is advertised on a thirty-two-story poster that wraps around the entire building. Donny's life-sized head can be seen from miles away, so I've yet to get lost on the way to work.

My "look up for the landmark" approach always falls apart, though, in places where you can't see the forest for the trees. I've been there, too. It calls for a different type of directions, a method I learned to put into practice early on in my life.

On one of our first international tours, my brothers and I went to Japan. We always learned some of our songs in the language of whatever country we were visiting by listening to them being sung over and over again, phonetically, by a person who speaks the language. Our welcome in Japan was incredibly warm. They were thrilled with our efforts to communicate through our music, and we were treated to the best that the country had to offer.

We stayed in the best geisha house, where we were taught the art of origami. We were served delicious Kobe beef, prepared traditionally. I was given the gift of a kimono, which was fitted to my size by a seamstress. My brothers were presented with an Akita puppy that Jay named Fuji. He was the offspring of the national grand champion. Fuji was even featured in *The Osmond Brothers* cartoon in the 1970s.

One of our hosts, not intending to be rude, studied the faces of my brothers and me. He had probably never seen such a large family. He smiled and said, "I will try to remember each of you by name but it will be hard. Americans all look alike to me."

One afternoon we were invited, along with other families, for a picnic to celebrate the strawberry harvest, which was at the peak of the season. The strawberries are not planted in fields in Japan. They are grown sideways, out of cement cubicles that are stacked at an angle one upon the other, about six containers high. This method keeps the strawberries from ever touching the ground so they are absolutely free of dirt or blemishes. You can pick them off of the plant and pop them directly into your mouth. The scent of strawberries in the air was only a preliminary tease to how delicious they tasted.

Our gracious host gave us each a cup of cream and sugar and told us to pick as many strawberries as we'd like to eat. Little did they know that a flock of Osmonds is capable of wiping out a whole crop of fresh strawberries in one sitting. Let me tell you, we permanently altered the feng shui in that garden.

The picnic was on the very edge of a forested area, so my brothers and I and some of the other children in the group decided to play a game of hide-and-seek. Even as a little girl I've always been pretty competitive, and sometimes my will to take home the prize overshadowed my common sense, and still does once in a while. Melon-colored Lucite heels, anyone?

Off I went, dashing into the woods, never looking back. I thought, "I'm for sure going to win this game. No one will ever find me here."

And I was so right. No one could find me, and after about fifteen minutes it occurred to me that I couldn't find them, either. I was lost. Every direction I looked presented the exact same scenery: trees, trees, trees, an occasional rock, and more trees. I could barely see the blue of the sky with the density of branches and leaves overhead.

In a panic, I started running as fast as I could, first in one direction and then the other, looking for any sign of a clearing. I would stop, momentarily, to try to hear the voices of other children, but my heart was pounding so hard I couldn't hear anything else. Tears started to burn my eyes, matching the sting of the scratches my bare legs were suffering from the ground brush and briars.

I was desperate for help, but when I called out to my brothers there was no answer.

Then I remembered a verse from the Bible that my mother would always say to us when we were afraid. It was from one of her favorites, Psalms (46:10): "Be still, and know that I am God."

I had been raised from infancy with the belief that God would never abandon me. I was told that any problems or concerns I had could be taken to God, and to listen for an answer by letting myself "be still."

Obviously, my own frantic attempts to get myself out of this forest were getting me nowhere, so with childlike faith I got on my knees and I prayed to God for a rescue. I asked that I be shown the way back to my brothers. I calmed down immediately and even grinned, thinking that God might say: "Are you sure???"

I said: "Yeah, I really do want to be with my brothers again." My bizarre sense of humor never left me, even though I was terrified. After all, I was the girl who would grow up to buy melon-colored Lucite heels.

A feeling of peace moved from my heart

to my head as I stayed perfectly still, listening. I knew I was being answered. A strong intuitive sense grew inside of me, a firm direction on which way to go to get out of the forest.

I stood up and began to walk confidently for a while. I had moments of fear as doubts swirled through my mind, wondering if I was only walking deeper and deeper into the woods. But when I pushed the doubts away, I could feel guidance, as though a gentle hand were on my back, urging me forward.

Finally, I heard the sound of people talking in the distance. I picked up my pace and knew I would soon be safe again. Actually, somehow I could tell that I had always been safe and protected. It was deeper than the knowledge that my family probably wouldn't drive off to do the next concert and leave me to perish in the woods. (Well, maybe Jimmy would have!) It was my first experience with truly trusting in God, and in the intuitive feelings that are the GPS of our soul, the voice that guides us if we can be still long enough to listen.

So, when I'm driving, I look up to find a landmark, whether it's a tall building or the mountain range or my brother's mug. When I am looking for true direction in any aspect of my life, I look up to find my one constant landmark, God. It's one of those things I "can't live without." I may briefly lose my way or need to "recalculate" my mistakes sometimes, but I rarely feel lost, at least not permanently.

As if it happened an hour ago, I can still remember saying "Thank you" to God when I saw the clearing and my brothers coming toward me with strawberry-stained grins.

One of them ran up and tagged me. "You're it."

The game had been changed, but so had I.

FAKE IT WHEN YOU CAN'T MAKE IT

Here's me "faking it" that I can keep up with the professional dancers in the Donny and Marie Fla-mingo *show!*

Photo by: Cashman Photography

51

I faked a pot roast. I had to. It was that or not come through on my promise to my kids.

I had told my daughter Rachael, who was then thirteen, and her sisters and brothers that I'd make their favorite meal: pot roast, potatoes, and carrots. It was the opening night of the school play *You're a Good Man, Charlie Brown.* Rachael was playing Lucy.

Suddenly it was already four p.m. and I still had to pick up my four-year-old from her tap-dance lessons, order cleats for my eleven-year-old football player, stop by the office to sign a contract, and retrieve my altered jacket from my seamstress to wear on QVC the next evening.

I ran into a grocery store to see what I could do instead of actually cooking. When I saw the woman behind the meat counter in her white lab-type coat I called out, "Help! Can you help me???" as if she were an emergency room technician. She seemed perfectly calm as she assisted me in finding two precooked pot roasts and then pointed me in the direction of fingerling microwavable potatoes. I take it I wasn't the first mom to assail her like a maniac for her storehouse of supper shortcut suggestions.

The trick in faking cooking is to hide the packaging. I pushed it to the bottom of the trash bag. After I microwaved all of the food, I even dumped it into a roaster pan and put it in the oven on low, enough to make the aroma fill the kitchen.

I had to fake the pot roast because I had also promised Rachael that I would find two wigs for the school play: one for her, as Lucy, and another for her good friend, who was playing Sally. I was optimistic that it wouldn't be complicated, but as it turns out, wig stores don't stock hair that makes women look like comic strip characters.

Okay, so I had to fake the wigs, too. I had the clerk box up whatever dark brown wig and blond wig were available for the least amount of money. I ran into the bookstore next door and grabbed a *Peanuts* book from the shelves and took it with me to my regular hairdresser.

As soon as I pushed open her salon door and saw her standing behind her chair with scissors and a comb, I called out, "Help! Can you help me???"

She very calmly opened up the two packages. The brunette hair looked like Joan Collins's hair on *Dynasty,* and the blond hair looked like Charo, circa 1969. I pushed the "Charlie Brown" book in her direction. "I need Lucy and Sally. Is there a chance?"

"Give me an hour," she said.

"I only have thirty minutes! I have a pot roast in the oven!"

"Okay," she said, taking up the challenge. "You know, you don't want to dry out those precooked roasts." She winked at me.

I take it I wasn't the first mom to throw polyester wigs at her like a maniac who needed a miracle.

I had to fake the wigs because I had also promised to be in the school auditorium thirty minutes before the play started to save seats for about fifteen extended family members.

As it turned out, by the time I got the wigs to the school dressing room, it was already thirty minutes before curtain time, and I still had to go home and get Rachael and the other kids.

I had to fake being able to save seats, too.

I looked at the people starting to enter the auditorium and saw a good friend of mine who was coming by herself to support my daughter in her school play. As soon as I saw her walking toward the door with her program in her hand, I shouted across the parking lot to her.

"Help! Can you help me???"

She turned, startled, and started jogging toward me, thinking I was in dire trouble.

"What is it?" she asked. "One of the kids? Are you ill?" Then she read my face. "You want me to save seats," she said knowingly.

"See how well we know each other!" I said, delighted. "I need fifteen."

"Okay," she said. She very calmly took stock of what she was wearing. "I've got two socks, a belt, my purse, three tissues, my program, a jacket, and my sunglasses case that I can use to hold seats. I can lay my body across the other four."

I take it I wasn't the first mom to ask her like a maniac to strip down to mark out a territory.

When I walked back through the front door of my house, my kids were finishing up their pot roast dinner.

Rachael hugged me. "Mom, that was so good! Your best one ever!"

"Wait until you see how cute the wigs are," I said to her.

I roused everyone from the table as I

popped a baby carrot into my mouth to tide me over. "Hurry! Get in the car. The play starts in twenty minutes."

My seat-saving friend in the school auditorium, who was almost down to her bra and Spanx, was relieved to see me after her hectic half hour of answering questions like "Excuse me! Is this gum wrapper saving this chair?"

When the extended family members entered the auditorium five minutes before the curtain, I was smiling and waving from the row of saved chairs. My children were happy from their favorite "homemade" meal, and the audience clapped when they saw how much Lucy's hair looked like Lucy's hair.

As a parent, it's important for me to keep my promises. I can keep almost every promise as long as there are other busy women in this world — women who know what the demands of being a mom are like, who multitask as often as they breathe, who can see what's needed and jump in, no explaining, no complaining. Busy women who I can count on to help me fake it when I can't make it.

I'd Rather Play the Toilet

That's right. Donny plays keyboards. Wayne plays guitar. I thought I had it bad playing the marimba, but my poor mom had to play the hot iron every day.
Osmond Family Archive

I was playing guitar onstage, finally! It's what I always really wanted to do . . . when I was *twelve.* Not anymore. I was certain the huge projection screens looming behind me were capturing a close-up of my fingers on the strings. Or, more likely, I was being caught with my fingers *off* the strings. I can only play four chords semi-well: G, C, D, and A-minor, the only ones I had the chance to learn as "a minor." Oh, and Dolly Parton had taught me once how to bar chords, when we shared a backstage area on the country music circuit in the mid-1980s. She had learned that technique so she could play guitar and also keep her beautiful long fingernails. Smart woman.

That's the extent of my six-string virtuosity.

I couldn't even turn sideways to hide my minimal playing skills without being caught on camera. My brothers thought it would be cool to film this concert from all directions: all 360 degrees. As men, they don't realize that this idea is every woman's worst nightmare. It's like being trapped in a department store dressing room with magnifying mirrors covering every wall. When your image is on a twenty-five-foot megatron screen, one-half inch of arm flab can look like a sail in the America's Cup.

We were in London, at a sold-out concert at the O2 arena. Twenty-five thousand fans had come to celebrate the Osmonds' fiftieth anniversary in show business. (I haven't been around quite that long yet. Donny has, though!)

A few weeks before, when we were rehearsing in Utah, I asked my brother Wayne for some quick pointers on the guitar because he actually does know how to play. He was also the main reason I didn't get to play as a teenager.

My parents invested the money we first made performing as children back into practical skills that we could use onstage. They hired great choreographers, voice teachers, and music arrangers. When it came to teaching us to play instruments, my parents devised a system that would be money-savvy and also simplify our daily calendars. They sent each of us to take lessons on a different instrument, and then we would come home and teach our instrument to everyone else. Wayne got to study guitar. Jay played drums. Alan learned the saxophone. Donny specialized in keyboards. My poor brother Merrill was responsible for learning to play the banjo. This did not score him points with teenage girls, whose only association with the banjo was *The Beverly Hillbillies* theme song. Merrill's pain only increased when we toured Japan and learned that "banjo" sounded very close to "benjo," the Japanese word for toilet. After that, every time he would practice his banjo, at least one of us felt compelled to stroll by and make a flushing sound.

I thought Merrill had it pretty bad, until it was my turn to learn an instrument. I chose the guitar. Guitars were the "it" instrument for girls. Joni Mitchell and Carly Simon had led the way in the sixties. Nancy Wilson of Heart made the guitar look like great fashion in the seventies. Even Betty, the blonde on *The Archies* cartoon series, could cook. When I told my mother that I wanted to play the guitar, she put her arm around my shoulders. "We already have a guitar player, which is Wayne. We need someone to play the marimba. And that can be you."

For a moment or two, I thought Mother using the word "can" left the door open for discussion on the issue, until I saw the faraway look on her face. I knew she was visualizing the possibilities for our Vegas Christmastime show. She was imagining a marquee on the famous Las Vegas Strip that read:

MARIE OSMOND — PLAYS THE
MARIMBA — COME HEAR
SLEIGH RIDE! NOT JUST TWO MAL-
LETS, BUT FOUR!

There was no shortage of reasons I did *not* want to learn to play this cumbersome Latin American folk instrument.

For those of you who are not up to speed on your popular Latin American percussion, the marimba is in the idiophone family of instruments. Yes, idiophone. Not a good self-esteem builder for a young girl. How close to the word "idiot" can you get? And the siblings in the idiophone family are the xylophone and wood blocks (used for horse hoof sounds). We all know how often teenage girls like to impress boys by replicating the sound of a trotting Clydesdale. Please! A marimba was not cool. I would rather play the toilet like Merrill.

Despite all of my legitimate reasons why the marimba was not for me, my mother could not be swayed from her vision. Days later, I was standing next to a woman who played the best marimba in all of Las Vegas. She was the top teacher in the area and my mother, in her excitement, had signed me up for lessons with her. I was at an awkward age, and this was certainly an awkward instrument to have to learn.

At about the third lesson, while I was still in pain from the thought of playing anything onstage, let alone a huge log cabin on wheels, the teacher instructed me to put some "feeling" into my playing. I guess she meant some feeling other than embarrassment.

My mother watched me practice from a chair at the side of the room. She looked on intently and then I heard her whisper loudly: "More eyes, Marie. More eyes!" She always loved the silent movies with the ingénues and their expressive eyes. I tried to tell her that . . . since the invention of sound recording . . . all that eye batting was unnecessary and way over the top.

In this case, though, she had a point. I hadn't looked up from the keys once because I was so worried that I might hit the wrong note. My mother wanted me to stop being concerned about individual notes and start to enjoy playing. I knew I would never live up to her expectations. I couldn't even use the words "marimba" and "enjoy" in the same sentence.

My mother thought I would eventually grow to love the marimba. It never happened. I dreaded every lesson, struggled through every song, and used to hope that some heavy lighting fixture would "accidentally" fall from the stage ceiling and send my marimba into oblivion.

London's O2 was only one stop on our twenty-five-date tour with the fiftieth-anniversary show. Hundreds of hours of technical planning, phone calls with venue owners, hiring of musicians and choreographers, creating light and sound designs, and scheduling with road managers had gone into the tour. Add to that list the countless hours coordinating all of us Osmonds for rehearsal time, along with the band and backup singers. It was a massive effort of love on everyone's part.

I knew it was time to stop thinking about my fingers on the strings of the guitar and the giant screens behind me, and change my focus to connecting with the audience. After all, they didn't buy a ticket expecting to see Joan Jett rock the house on a Gibson double cut-away. They had come to see my brothers and me. They had come to sing along to our many hits, to have a great time, and, in a very overwhelming way that we will never forget, share the love.

For fifty years, they have bought our records, attended our concerts, funded our star on the Hollywood Walk of Fame, written to us, cheered us, and become our "family of fans." As I looked out at their faces from the stage, many seemed to have mixed emotions about this concert. I believe they were the same emotions my brothers and I were experiencing. We had realized that this might be the very last tour in which all of us would appear together onstage. I say "might" because I almost never say "never." I've learned that whenever I say "never," something comes along to say: "Oh, yeah? Guess what!"

Except I'm sure I can say "never" about one thing: I will *never, ever* again play the marimba.

THE ONES WHO REALLY LIVE HAPPILY EVER AFTER

I had my first child twenty-six years ago. It was also the birth year of the charity I cofounded, Children's Miracle Network, which watches more than 17 million of my other kids every year.

Photo Courtesy of Children's Miracle Network

A plate of tuna fish sandwiches was how it all began. A kitchen table. A yellow legal pad and pencil. Eating lunch that afternoon at my brother Alan's home were John Schneider (yes, *Dukes of Hazzard* John), myself, and a small group of very talented businesspeople. I've read various claims that the omega oils in fish really boost brain-power. I'd have to say it was doing its job that afternoon, because at that table in the fall of 1981, the idea for Children's Miracle Network was born.

At the twenty-fifth-anniversary celebration in 2008, someone in the press asked me how John and I got involved in cofounding the charity. I think I answered that John is like a brother to me. Which is true. However, it's also true that we did date once. Okay, maybe twice or more. He asked me out soon after the *Donny and Marie* show went off the air, and just as the *Dukes of*

Hazzard was a fresh hit show. I went from four years of performing with Been Duped (Donny!) to dating Bo Duke. What a transition.

John was and still is handsome, funny, and kind-hearted, a combination that's not always easy to find. However, by the time he asked me out on a date, my heart was already pretty occupied by Steve, the Brigham Young University basketball star whom I was also starting to see. That story continued with a picture-book wedding, but didn't end with happily ever after, like we had both hoped. By the time this Children's Miracle Network lunch meeting took place, I'm certain that John Schneider and I were no longer dating. I mean, no one eats tuna fish when they're trying to flirt. Right?

Our topic of the day was: How could we help more kids who are physically challenged, sick, or injured? And how would we decide which cause needed the most help? There were hundreds of causes, all important, each needing funding for research and various treatments.

Years before, my parents had established the Osmond Foundation, a charity to help hearing-impaired children, because my two oldest brothers, Virl and Tom, were born deaf.

If a newborn appeared to be healthy in the 1940s, he was sent home with the mother with no further tests. Vision and hearing were only routinely tested when a child entered public school. My mother had to make the scary discovery with her first two babies on her own. Virl, the oldest, was showing some signs of speech problems as a preschooler, but she thought Tom was merely a quiet baby.

My parents had just moved to Ogden, Utah, and my father was devoting eighteen-hour days to setting up a real estate and insurance business. To keep my brothers entertained, he built them a little sandbox in the backyard. Mother told me that she was calling to them one day to come in the house and realized that only Virl looked up at her. Tommy never responded at all.

After having them tested and finding out that Virl had less than sixty percent hearing and that Tom was almost totally deaf, doctors recommended that they be placed in an institution as soon as they reached school age. This was where my mother put her foot down. Not the first or last time, either! (I think I inherited the best of her headstrong qualities.) She couldn't bear the thought of having her babies live away from her. As devastating as the news was to her, by the time she arrived home, she had started making a plan.

Day by day she taught them to speak. She would put her face near to theirs and pronounce words, letting them feel her throat as she spoke. She devised a way for them to hear speech through earphones and a record player. My father painted the kitchen walls with blackboard paint and my mother became their teacher. They were given tap-dance lessons to feel rhythm, and were both so good they ended up teaching the rest of my brothers to dance. She and my father not only taught my two oldest brothers to function well in a hearing world, but they taught the rest of their kids the ultimate blessings that come with helping other people. When my brothers Alan, Wayne, Merrill, and Jay first started singing at professional events as very young boys, it was to raise money to buy the best-quality hearing aids for their older brothers. Later, the funds went to the Osmond Foundation to help other deaf children.

My parents strongly believed that philanthropy was not only something we could do in our spare time but something that was to be part of our weekly schedules. It was, in their view, as important a time commitment as finding time to eat. One nourished the body, the other the spirit.

Almost every day during the seventies, a crowd of teenage girl fans would stand vigil outside of whatever house, apartment, studio, or hotel we happened to be occupying in order to catch a glimpse of my brothers. They would always call out, "Hi, Mother Osmond!!!" whenever she would enter or exit. I guess because they always called her "Mother," she felt she had the go-ahead to advise them in the same way she did all of her children. I would sometimes see her walk over to the fence or sidewalk where the girls lined up, and with a broad smile on her face and gentleness in her voice, say, "Stop wasting your time, girls. Think of how much good you could be doing to help other people with all these hours you spend standing here. Go be of service by reading to the blind, or helping out a handicapped child. You could be working in a food pantry or visiting the elderly. Now, get going, girls. Then report back to me on what you accomplished!"

I know quite a few girls did report back to my mother over the years how she had changed their lives, often by her encouragement to "not waste a moment of this precious life."

The idea for Children's Miracle Network,

scribbled out on that legal pad over twenty-five years ago, was to help as many kids as possible by supporting the hospitals that cared for them. Through funds raised by individuals, media outlets, and wonderful corporate sponsorship, as well as through the dedication of amazing doctors, nurses, and researchers who have donated countless hours of their time, Children's Miracle Network is now able to provide state-of-the-art care and facilities to 17 million children every year. To date, $3.4 billion worth of free medical care has been given away to families who need help in making sure their child receives the best possible chance at life.

A couple of years ago, I was stopped in an airport by a darling man who wanted to shake my hand.

"I wanted to say hello and to thank you," he said shyly. "I was a Children's Miracle Network Champion about twenty years ago. I was fourteen then, and had undergone three rounds of chemotherapy for lymphoma."

I'm always thrilled to meet one of the Champion kids again.

"Then I was bald from the chemo," he continued. "Now I'm just getting bald from middle age!"

I told him, "I'll be smiling about this success story for weeks."

The money CMN has raised has helped millions of families. And for me, the opportunity to be in the presence of these incredible children over the years has helped me in countless ways as well: teaching me, expanding my thinking, increasing my gratitude. I've heard this same sentiment from everyone who works with Children's Miracle Network, from the most brilliant surgeon to the high school volunteers who help out by doing fund-raising dance-a-thons.

I've never once met a sick or injured child who had a "why me?" outlook on life, even when their condition appeared to be incurable. One small boy, whom I'll call Blake, was no exception.

I met Blake and his parents during a radio interview about the Children's Miracle Network fund-raising gala at a Florida resort a couple of years ago. Blake has brittle bone disease, and though he was seven years old at the time, he was about the size of a three-year-old due to the disease. He wore Harry Potter–type glasses along with his adorable grin, and had his wheelchair decorated with various stickers, mostly Disney characters. It was not the first time my heart has been captured, but when he burst into giggles at my one and only pirate joke (What's a pirate's favorite letter of the alphabet? R-r-r-r-r-r-r-r-r-r-r-r), I just had to hijack his wheelchair and run away with him.

With his parents in close pursuit, we got as far as the resort gift store, which was featuring toys from the latest *Pirates of the Caribbean* movie.

"I want to get you something fun. Pick out a toy just for you," I told him as we took a tour of everything available.

After doing two laps of the entire store, Blake reached up to a rack to choose a plastic pirate's sword that lit up and made swashbuckler sounds. He held it up for his parents to see.

It was only an inexpensive little toy, so I insisted that Blake pick out another gift to go along with it. I showed him around to the more extravagant *Pirates of the Caribbean* play sets. We looked at scallywag hats and board games, ships in bottles and pirate watches. Though his eyes lit up and he seemed excited about each new selection, he would always return them to the shelf.

As we circled back to where we started, Blake took one more plastic sword off the rack, handed it to me, and said, "Thank you very much."

"Pick out something else you really want," I said, hanging the sword back on the rack. "I'm already getting you a sword like this. Remember?"

Blake dropped his voice to a whisper. I bent my head down to hear him.

"I know," he said. "But Alex doesn't have one."

Confused, I looked up at Blake's parents.

Blake's mom explained. "Alex is his friend at the children's hospital. He's a five-year-old being treated for an inoperable brain tumor. Blake always makes sure Alex never feels left out."

I'm often left speechless by these children, usually because their pure intentions leave me swallowing tears.

Perhaps it is their challenges, faced in their few years on earth, that give them such clarity about what matters most, along with a deep understanding that "happily ever after" is now.

I'm grateful that Children's Miracle Network has given families access to financial and emotional support, technology, and the best research available, so they don't have to figure it out on their own the way my mother did with Virl and Tom. Mostly, though, I'm overwhelmed by the life-changing blessings these children give to all of us who work with and for them. I'm always reminded that some special spirits can, in seven short years, walk that enlightened path that takes most of us seven decades or more to journey.

A busy manager from one of our major sponsors, who was attending the Children's Miracle Network celebration for the first time, summed it up perfectly for me. She had spent the day meeting each of the Champion children, one representing each state, the Canadian provinces, and the UK, and spending five or ten minutes with each of them.

As I posed for a picture with her, I had to ask, "What did you think of our Champion kids?"

"Here's the manager coming out in me," she said, with a wink. "Just like with my employees, I hope these kids don't compare notes about what I said to them."

It stopped me for a moment, wondering what she had possibly said that she was worried about.

"I'm afraid the kids might think I was being insincere, but I truly meant what I said to each one," she continued. Tears spilled onto her blouse.

"I'm sure it's fine," I consoled her. "What

did you say?"

Her eyes scanned the noisy room full of children being helped by parents and volunteers to get ready for the evening event, where each child gets an award and a standing ovation as a Champion.

"I said: You will probably never remember me, but I will never, ever forget you."

I understand, completely.

HOT PROPERTY: GREAT OPEN FLOOR PLAN, FULL MOUNTAIN VIEWS

This was the front of the Christmas card I sent out in 2005. Talk about your warm holiday wishes!

Osmond Family Archive

The floor plan was perfect; the kitchen was big enough for all of us; it had bright, spacious bedrooms, plenty of bathrooms, a fenced-in backyard for kids and pets, and a large finished basement, just right for my teenagers to have their own space. We had been living bunk-bed style in the house we bought in Orem, Utah, when there were only five of us. Now there were nine of us, with number ten on the way with the upcoming arrival of Abigail that September.

I was even able to acquire some gorgeous pieces of furniture from the woman who was selling her house. I was astonished at her willingness to part with everything so easily. She shrugged about their significance, waving them off as if they were pesky cats trying to entangle her feet, limiting her movement. I wasn't sure why she was being so generous with her belongings, but I wasn't going to question it, either.

For the first time in my life, I was going to be able to have a full room for my home office. "Office" was my shortened name for the room that would be used for my doll display, crafting, scrapbooking, computer work, rubber stamping, gift wrapping, photo framing, painting, sculpting, quilting, sewing, journal writing, reading, meditating, archiving, storing memorabilia, making private phone calls, getting away, taking a deep breath, collecting myself, and finding some peace. (Whew!)

I loved the space, which was by itself at one end of the house, over the two-car garage. I was crazy about it all, from the floor space, large enough to lay out a queen-sized quilt, to my black leather couches, to the vaulted ceilings with what seemed to be mile-high windows. I had enclosed glass shelving holding many of my porcelain dolls, all of them limited editions. Thirty years of my personal journals were stored in cabinets near my desk.

I saved an area for things my mother had left to me: her favorite scriptures, books, photo albums, an antique sewing machine, embroidered pillowcases and tatted handkerchiefs, business ideas written out in notebooks, a set of her treasured china, and other sweet remembrances of her. I also found a way to store most of the memorabilia of my career: framed photos, platinum records, awards and letters from presidents, along with boxes of gifts from fans.

I declared it a kid-free zone, which my children seemed to interpret as "free to any kid, any time." They instantly began to inhabit my sanctuary, turning the couches into trampolines, adjusting their skateboard wheels on top of my sewing table, adding glitz to their jeans pockets and my pretty oak tabletop, and teaming up for pickup games of Nerf basketball. When I opened my knitting bag and found a hamster wheel with a gerbil still using it, I decided the door needed a lock.

The first week the office door was latched, my youngest son, then two and a half, managed to break in and superglue my heavy crystal elephant (a gift from when I performed *The King and I* on Broadway) to my brand-new end table. To follow in her brother's footsteps, Abigail, at around the same age, jimmied the door and decided to personalize my computer screen with some purple passion nail polish and about ten "Whassup???" stickers. I'll tell you what's up!!!!!

This is one of the continuing mysteries of childhood that really should be scientifically studied. How is it that children who find it impossible to close any of their own cabinets, closets, or drawers until they are about nineteen years old can, at twenty-seven months of age, open any and all "kid-proof" locks with complete ease?

One day in September of 2005, I was in my office thinking about my mother. She would have loved a room to call her own, let alone a room this size. With nine of us kids, her personal space was, at best, a corner of the kitchen counter or a small desk crammed at the very end of a hallway between bedroom doors. She never complained about a lack of private time, though I think she must have craved it. I was reading one of her journals from thirty-five years before and came upon this entry: "It's eleven p.m. I can't seem to get these children to go to bed!" It made me laugh, first, and then broke my heart a bit. As much as she loved us, she must have felt she never had time to just be "Olive." (Olive is my true first name, as well. Thank heavens I've always gone by Marie, my middle name. I don't think the *Donny and Olive* show would have held much punch.) As I sat on my couch, looking down at her sweet handwriting, I wished my office could have been hers.

The very next day, I was wishing it could

be mine, again. My room and almost everything in it was totally gone in less than an hour. I was driving with Patty and my two youngest daughters to deliver a speech at a girls' camp in the Angeles National Forest when I got the call.

It all happened quickly, I was told. Though the cause was never really verified, it was assumed that a very young curious child with a fireplace lighter had set a broom ablaze in the garage. Frightened of getting into trouble, the child dropped the broom and came into the house.

When the fire ignited the gas tanks of the two WaveRunners stored in the garage, the flames spread rapidly up the back wall. Neighbors who saw the billowing smoke ran into the house, first rescuing the children and also waking up their father, Brian, who was napping upstairs. My son Michael called 9-1-1 as my neighbors joined forces to carry whatever belongings could be saved out to the lawn.

Though smoke damaged every room of the house as it was suctioned through the air-conditioning vents, my quick-thinking neighbors did manage to save most of my favorite framed family photos, artwork, and antique furniture. What was impossible to save was my office and almost every single thing in it, as the fire burned through the roof of the garage and reduced the walls of my room to charred embers.

Patty was driving along the highway, looking over at me in shock every now and then as I described the damage to her after the phone call.

"What do you want to do?" she asked. "Should we cancel this talk today? Should we drive to the airport? Do you want me to keep the kids? Go with you? Where will you stay? Who's going to help you?" Patty's a person who takes action immediately once a plan is in place. Who doesn't need a friend to help you think in a crisis?

This time, however, my thinking was very clear. My babies were all safe, which was all I really needed to know, and I had a commitment to keep. I did my talk to a group of about one hundred young women.

Looking out at their teenaged faces and their attempts to be so mature and independent in attitude and fashion reminded me of my own trial run at being a grown-up, and how uncool it really was. In fact, it was blazing hot!

It was the first time my parents were able to take a vacation together without any children along. My brother Jay had surprised them with a gift of a cruise and a guided tour of the Holy Land. We had convinced them to enjoy some vacation time, as Donny and I were in our late teens and Jimmy was always reliable, right from the start. He had already toured Japan and was being offered a television show there at the career-savvy age of fourteen. If the three of us could handle hosting national television shows, we figured we could certainly handle running a house on our own for ten days.

One of my girlfriends had come over to stay with us while my parents were out of town, and one day we decided to fry some hamburgers. As teenagers who were terrified of fat, or anything edible that wasn't cooked to death, we decided to cook our burgers well, well, well done. Think Cajun before it was cool! I am sure we imagined that high heat would burn off the calories before we even ate them!

As we stood there talking, the top of the pan burst into flames from the overheated grease that had pooled around the burgers.

My girlfriend screamed and Donny came running in from the living room.

He jumped into action as soon as he saw the leaping flames.

"I've got it!" he yelled, grabbing a dish towel and wrapping it around the handle of the pan. He jerked the pan up off the stove and started toward the sink.

"Wait!" I shouted, afraid of what he was about to do. But it was too late. As he hurried across the room, grease slopped over the edge of the pan, sending flames to the floor. This probably wouldn't have been a big crisis, but it was the seventies, when people carpeted their kitchens. (Ugly. No two ways around it.) The carpet began to burn.

As I stood there in disbelief, Donny tossed the pan into the sink and turned the faucet on full blast.

The fire flared up from the sink and ignited the bottom of the kitchen cupboards.

I grabbed the family-sized box of baking soda from the pantry and ripped it apart to spread on the smoldering carpet before the flames could spread farther, while Donny slapped at the cupboards with a wet towel. When the fires were finally out we stood speechless in disbelief. I was sick to my stomach for the rest of the day, so upset that I had ruined the brand-new remodeling my parents had done in the kitchen.

My parents arrived home from Jerusalem about three days later. I can't remember feeling worried that they would be angry. It probably would have made me feel better if they had been. I was mostly concerned about their disappointment at my irresponsibility — I looked for anger and disappointment on their faces when I showed them the kitchen, but it wasn't there. What I saw was gratitude that we had been protected from physical harm.

I think, in their wisdom, my parents knew that I had punished myself enough. Of course, they left the hole in the carpet. I always thought they chose to do that as an unspoken reminder to be more careful, but now I wonder if it was because it was so ugly that it was discontinued, and they were unable to match it again.

I knew that my child who started the garage fire would be feeling the same way.

I prayed that when I stepped off the plane the next day and took that child in my arms I would have the same expression on my face that I saw on my parents' faces.

When I arrived back in Utah and saw the house and the gaping hole that used to be my office, I had the most unexpected reaction. Though it was shocking visually, I was more shocked by what I was feeling: it was a strange relief.

I had fallen way behind on keeping a scrapbook for each child and had been feeling guilty about that. Now I could help them figure out a way to make their own.

My journals were all destroyed, but between my dyslexia and my exhaustion when writing them right before I fell asleep, I doubt anyone could have read them anyway. The memorabilia from my career wasn't necessary; I still had the good memories without having to store so much stuff. Though I felt twinges of pain about losing some of it, like one-of-a-kind photographs of Donny and me with John Wayne, Groucho Marx, and Lucille Ball, I've never been one to hang on to past glory days.

The only loss I felt more deeply was for some of the items my mother had left to me. As I was shoving aside some splintered and charred shelves, I found one small three-ring notebook that had survived the fire. It was a sketchbook in which she had drawn dress designs for my upcoming dolls. Her handwriting was undamaged. It made me laugh. I wondered if she had somehow saved it for me, sending the message not to cry about the past but to plan for the future! As she would say: "Don't live in the pasture!"

That evening, the ten of us crammed into two hotel rooms, the girls in one room and the boys in the other. There's nothing like trying to make oatmeal in a tiny hotel coffeemaker for hungry children. We had to do some power shopping to quickly replace school clothing and supplies for the kids for their first week of school. About a week later, we found a house to rent while ours was being emptied and then rebuilt. In an ironic twist, the rental was a very small house and we had to figure out how to live close together again. Each night, my children would pile into bed with me and we would read our scriptures and tell stories.

When the holidays approached, I happened to cross paths with one of the firefighters who came to the rescue that September day. He had taken a picture of the fire on his cell phone and it was the first time I got to see the severity of the blaze.

Looking at the photo, my Christmas card idea for 2005 came to me. I asked him if he could send me the picture by e-mail.

All my friends and business associates received the same holiday greeting from me that year. On the front of the card is the photograph showing firefighters preparing to hose down the side of the house. An inferno is leaping out of the windows and pouring from the garage door. I framed the photo in a red ribbon and holly berries design. Inside the card I had printed the following greeting:

A Special Christmas Offer:

10 brand-new carols from the Osmond-Blosil Holiday Songbook:

"It's Beginning to Look a Lot Like Crispness"
"What Charred Is This?"
"Spray Ride"
"Over the Rear Wall and Through the Wood"
"Here Comes Suzy Smokebake"
"Siren Night"
"Up on the Roof Top Reindeer Roast"
"Away in a Danger"
"Hark the Herald Angels Singe"
"Douse the Halls"

Order NOW and receive a bonus track:
"All I Want for Christmas Is My Two Front Rooms."

Friends and family all responded with a lot of enthusiasm when they got the card in the mail. Some people even told me that it gave them an open door to laugh about their own troubles from the past year, too.

When we finally moved back into the house in the early spring, I was, again, surprised by my unexpected reaction: sorrow. Though it was still a perfect house, I was starting to sense that it was never going to be a happy family home. I thought about the woman who had sold it to me. She had told me that she was going through a painful divorce and had to reprioritize. Her children were grown and she had no need for a big house and a lot of belongings. She'd never expected to be alone at this point in her life, but she was bravely making choices for her future. I distinctly remember the expression on her face, both weary and hopeful. I was starting to recognize the same expression on my face looking back at me from the mirror. A crisis often tests a marriage. I've watched many couples bond more closely through tough times, but that had not happened with my marriage. The inconvenience of having to readjust our lives because of the fire served to magnify for me all of the countless ways we were no longer in sync with each other and hadn't been for years. The continuous attempts to repair our relationship always seemed to crumble into cinders. The smoke had now cleared, literally and figuratively, and I knew I had to look closely at my marriage and measure the damage, carefully.

Bloomin' Cactus

My greatest happiness has always come from being a mother.

Osmond Family Archive

Brian was a funny man. His dry sense of humor could make me laugh. He could also be ridiculous just for the sake of it: wearing a grass skirt and doing a hula dance for a crowd of tourists; or the time he dressed up as a giant spotted dog for Halloween.

I'm a woman who loves to laugh. Brian's quick wit won me over the first night I met him. We had come separately to a party hosted by my brother Jay. I was divorced from Steve and starting to acclimate myself to the thought of raising my son as a single mom.

My parents had taught me to never give up. It was a motto my brothers and I applied to every aspect of our lives. Steve and I had made several attempts to go back and make our very young marriage work, but it failed. I was being scrutinized in the tabloids and the paparazzi seemed to show up wherever I went. I was emotionally exhausted. I wanted to sit and cry the days away and, at first, I did.

One morning I was in my parents' kitchen, focused on my hopeless situation, asking my mother the one constant question of the heartbroken: "How will I ever get over this?"

She had been kind, sympathetic, and supportive about whatever choice I thought I should make from the first sign of my marital problems. On this particular day, however, I think she was worried that I was falling into the snare of self-pity, a habit that can become way too comfortable if it settles in as a way of life. Neither of my parents ever had any tolerance for a "poor me" attitude.

"Marie!" my mother said firmly. "You have to dry your eyes, gather yourself together, and get on with it. You have a child who needs a happy mother."

I wasn't expecting that from my own mother and it made me more upset. My tears soon turned to anger when she added, "So figure out a way to be happy. Pull yourself up by the bootstraps and grow up."

I was so mad that she wouldn't sympathize with me, I could barely see straight. But within minutes I started to perceive the true situation. My mother was right. It was good shock therapy and it worked. You can't stand by and let someone physically die if you know you can stop the bleeding; and she wasn't going to stand by and watch my will to live drain out of me. She didn't want my son to grow up with a negative-thinking mother.

I applied my mom's sage advice and turned my focus to my son and my work, and little by little it took my mind off of my emotional pain. The hurt and the anger about my divorce were crowded out by the joy of being a mother to a darling baby. He was the best gift. Still is.

At this party, it was Jay's intention to introduce me to another guest with hopes that it would spark a bit of interest between us. He had invited Steve Young, who, at that time, was the star quarterback for Brigham Young University. Steve's amazing football career has since garnered him MVP awards and an induction into the Pro Football Hall of Fame. He's got a Hall of Fame heart, too, and works extensively for Children's Miracle Network. We've been friends for over two decades.

That evening, though, I stayed a safe distance from getting to know him. I was telling myself that it was too early for me to start dating again, but my reluctance was more likely because he embodied rising success and I was feeling like a failure. Then again, maybe it was only his name. After all, I was still recovering from my first love, and now ex-husband, Steve.

Brian was there at the same party. He didn't seem at all intimidating to me. And he was funny. He wanted to become a music producer. He belonged to my church. The rest is history. They say fashion trends recycle every twenty years. In my case, history did, too.

In December of 2007, almost one year after I filed for divorce from Brian, I was getting ready to shoot a commercial for NutriSystem. The NutriSystem representatives seemed extremely happy with my success at weight loss, and the outpouring of compliments by the crew, associates, and friends had me wondering . . . what the heck were they thinking about my size before?????

Anyway, one of my favorite people in the world was doing my hair. She has been in my life since I was fifteen years old, beginning when she was the hairstylist on the *Donny and Marie* show. She knows me so well. She's heard all of my hopes, dreams, issues, heartbreaks, and headaches for years. I've listened to hers, too, and always appreciate her subtle ways of teaching me through her own experiences. Now, as an adult, I count on her wisdom more than ever, and on this day she had another gem.

We were talking about divorce and its reasons. Having been through three divorces herself, she said: "In a second relationship I think women look for what was missing from the first marriage. Often it blinds us to seeing the complete picture because we're so happy to experience what we had lacked for so long."

I know that was true of me with Brian. Laughter had been missing from my life for over a year following my first divorce, and Brian was like a buffet table of humor in the beginning of our relationship. I thought humor was the balm that would make everything better. I was a twenty-five-year-old woman who didn't step back long enough to see the big picture.

It was a rebound relationship in the most classic of ways, but I still tried to make it grow and work for years on end. I had always believed in the scriptural wisdom of being "equally yoked," and it was soon obvious the two of us were not. Nonstop domestic bliss is, of course, a fairy tale; but having the same priorities plays a huge part in a good marriage. More often than not, Brian and I weren't even on the same map, much less the same path.

Following the bleakest days of my experience with postpartum depression, during the second season of the *Donny & Marie* talk show, Brian and I separated for six months. Depression of any kind can bring a side effect that is impossible to ignore. It lowers your guard and magnifies whatever issues you might have submerged in self-denial. For women, depression often means that we can no longer rise to the occasion of making it look easy, cope with the struggles, or use any of our energy for keeping the peace. It is too draining to pretend to be happy. For me, this meant that I couldn't figure out a way to live with our massive differences anymore.

Brian moved back to our Utah home while I stayed with the children to finish out the television season in Los Angeles. I talked with a therapist to understand and work on my issues. When I saw Brian again, I felt he had made many changes as well. For the children's sake, above all, we felt highly motivated to try saving the marriage.

We got back together during the months I was writing my first book, *Behind the Smile.* At the time, I thought I was being optimistic when I wrote these words in one of the final chapters: "I still had fears about renewing the relationship. But, little by little, we let the walls down and chipped away at the awful fear that it would only be a matter of time before we fell into the patterns that had given us reason to separate."

But now I read within those words an intuitive sense of our future.

Following the house fire in the fall of 2005, I started to contemplate our situation with eyes that had been cleared of the smoke of blind hope: the structure was gone — what was left inside? I couldn't stand the possibility of my children coming from a broken home, but I also knew they were growing up with two parents in a broken relationship. I knew that had to be damaging in and of itself. I prayed continuously for an answer. And I desperately hoped that God would fix what was broken in my marriage, especially if I continued to try.

About a year later, I was touring with my *Magic of Christmas* show. Six of my children made a stage appearance to sing a family song with me. Jessica prefers to be behind the scenes, and she is great at stage managing. Michael organized the microphones and was a pinch-hit drummer. We had a great time, all crowded into one bus, traveling to a new city every day and performing at night. It's a lot of hard work, but when it's a holiday show, the audiences are always ready to have a great time and that joy reverberates onstage and is carried onto the bus. Brian started the tour with us, but didn't finish. It was clear to everyone that we were unhappy together. By the time the holidays were over, so was our living in the same house.

One afternoon, after Brian had left the tour, as I was putting on makeup for a show, I overheard my oldest son, Stephen, talking to his sisters about our marriage.

He said, "I really believe that you have to work at marriage. But I would rather make a good marriage really great than try to make a bad marriage good."

It was painful to hear my son's assessment of the marriage, but his honesty gave me a new perspective.

With respect to my parents' advice to never give up, I would now add my own experienced adage: "Never give up yourself in order to try to make someone else happy." It doesn't work. I know change is possible, but I've learned that it will only last if you want it for yourself, first. In good marriages, compromises are made so you can both stay happy, not just so the other person will stay happy.

After losing so many of my mom's sweet needlecrafts and handmade items in the house fire, I was devoted to keeping her Christmas cactus plant, which had survived any long-term damage, alive and well. My mother had such a green thumb and would sing and talk to her plants every morning. Every year her Christmas cactus rewarded her attention with a respectable number of blooms. When we left on the Christmas tour, I gave specific directions for the care of the cactus to a friend who was watching the house for us. Returning on Christmas Eve, I was so disappointed to find it pale and without a single blossom. It seemed to be matching my spirit of sorrow about the inevitability of my marriage ending. I thought over and over about my parents' marriage and how they not only loved each other, but walked the same path, strove to improve themselves together and separately, and always encouraged each other in all things. And in their closeness, they laughed. Every day.

In the weeks that followed, I had many sleepless nights, wondering if I was being wise. I knew that divorce couldn't resolve our relationship problems. We have seven children together, and many other choices would have to be made as a result of this one choice.

I felt that God's answer to my ongoing

plea for guidance was to remind me always of the gift of free agency. I was the one who had made the choice to be in the marriage, and now that I found my feet to the fire, it was for me to fix the mess. I wasn't going to be rescued. The only way I would ever learn and grow was to make the next decision on my own, too.

My heart was heavy and I wished I had my mother with me still. To say to me firmly: "Gather yourself together! You have children who need a happy mother."

Imagining her saying this to me suddenly gave me the clarity I needed. I would never be that happy mother if I stayed in my marriage. I would never be the best person I could be for my children or for myself. I knew I had my answer. The next morning I called an attorney and said I wanted to file for divorce. Though I knew it was right, I still longed for my mother to tell me that it would be okay, to give me encouragement.

I went downstairs, listening to the voices of my little children getting ready for school. As I turned into the kitchen and went to the refrigerator for the orange juice, something caught my eye. On that February morning, a new beginning was announcing itself once again. My mother's Christmas cactus had bloomed overnight and was

covered with dozens of bright fuchsia flowers.

NEEDLED

I'm wearing the diamond stud earrings my dad gave me for my sweet sixteen. If you use a magnifying glass you can see them.

Osmond Family Archive

I had to wait seven long years to get needled. I had asked for it every year for my birthday, starting at age eight, but my father didn't think that I was old enough to handle it. I couldn't figure out why it was such a big deal.

"It doesn't hurt," I tried to convince him at age ten. "It's fast. No blood."

"You might regret it," he told me. "You're still too young for those types of long-term decisions."

"Now they use a gun!" I pleaded with my dad when I turned thirteen. "They won't miss."

"When you're sixteen, you can decide," he told me. "Not before."

It could have been the words like "blood" and "gun" that bothered my father, a war vet, but I think it was more about what ear piercing would signify to him. His only daughter would no longer be a little girl.

So for me, and obviously also for my dad, having a teeny-tiny hole punched into each earlobe turned into a rite of passage, a bridge from girl to young woman.

Needle-less to say, in my own mind, I was already a full-grown woman by age twelve, and my sixteenth birthday seemed like a torturously long, almost eternal time to wait. I knew that I was going to forever love my pierced ears. I was right about that. I wear earrings every day. But I was wrong about the grown woman thing.

My teenagers have tried to talk me into accepting that getting a tattoo should be no big deal. Though it may be true that everyone seems to have one now, from the pre-school teachers to soccer coaches, I'm not crazy about the thought of any of my children having permanent dye injected into their skin with needles, no matter how old they are. They're my babies! I pampered that skin they're in.

I tried the most logical reason, sounding very much like my father: "Tattoos are permanent! What if you change your mind?"

They insisted that they never would.

"Tats will always be cool. I would never regret having one," they tried to tell me.

Did I have an answer for that: "When I was your age, everyone thought that wearing leg warmers with jeans and Let's Get Physical headbands would always, always be cool. Good thing they weren't permanently attached. Right?"

At this point, my daughter offered up one word that blew away my reasoning, unquestionably: eyeliner.

How could I defend my position about tattoos when I had not only one, but two? They have now faded away to nothing, but at one time you couldn't miss them. I had one on each eyelid. They were Cleopatra black. Tattooed eyeliner.

It seemed like the perfect solution at the time to an upcoming makeup dilemma. I was going to be one of the parents on a three-day rafting trip with my daughter's youth group. We would be sleeping in a tent overnight and could only take a small knapsack, one that wouldn't weigh down the raft. There would be no spare room for a makeup bag, and even if I could wear makeup, I knew I'd probably end up being dunked under water at some point.

I was telling this to a friend of mine who has a beautician's license.

"Look at my eyes," she said with some excitement. "It's tattooed eyeliner! I did it myself."

It looked really good on her.

"I never have to worry about being caught without makeup," she told me, "even on our houseboat on Lake Powell."

"I need that!" I told her. "It's the perfect solution to this rafting caper. I won't have to resort to using a permanent black Sharpie for my eyeliner."

That afternoon, after doing my radio show, I went to her house, where she was all set up and ready to go. She numbed my eyelids with some gel and got out a tiny microscopic syringe filled with dark ink. I think getting a tattoo on your arm or ankle must be a lot easier. I don't know about other people, but if you saw a needle coming toward your eyeball, you'd flinch! Right? And then flinch again! Not to mention the twitching. I mean, it's a NEEDLE, by my eyeball!!! It's a good thing my friend has such calm hands and meticulous aim. I could have ended up looking like Jack Sparrow (Johnny Depp) in the pirate movies. Arrrrrrrgh!

I loved the results, until the next morning, when I could no longer see the results. I couldn't see anything. My eyelids had swollen shut. Every eyelash follicle felt like a porcupine quill.

My beautician friend had warned me. She told me to go directly home, and lie flat for at least two hours while applying ice packs. But I had a slight problem with her advice. When you're wearing ice packs on your eyes you can't see what your kids are up to!

I had to get my four younger kids through dinnertime, shower time, story time, and finally bedtime. It was about five hours later by the time I got to lie down. I remembered the ice packs about two seconds before I drifted off into a deep sleep. I may have dreamed about ice packs, but that didn't help.

After the kids left for school in the morning, I decided to give my own "pupils" the cold treatment. I lay down with an ice bag on each eye. I had exactly twenty-four hours to look normal before grabbing a paddle and living the Hiawatha life for three days on a river.

About thirty minutes later my cell phone rang with a 9-1-1 call from another close girlfriend.

I picked up the phone to a long wail that I recognized from my own past.

"I can't take this," my girlfriend said. "My hormones are so out of control that I spent the night walking the floor. My heart is racing and I can't stop crying."

She wanted the name of the doctor who

helped me through my postpartum depression.

I could hear in her voice that she was in no shape to figure out how to get to any appointment.

"Hang on," I told her. "I'm coming for you. I'll take you to the clinic. You'll be okay."

The swelling in my eyes had gone down far enough to see to drive, even though my eyelids were so heavy that blinking felt like weight lifting.

"I can't go today!" my girlfriend cried over the phone. "I look like a wreck. You wouldn't believe how red and swollen my eyes are. Don't come for me. I'm not going."

I could tell she would only go downhill. She needed some attention.

"Listen," I said. "If I promise to look worse than you, will you go with me to the clinic?"

"You never look bad," she sobbed.

"Just come get in my car when I get there. Okay?" She agreed.

As soon as she got in the car and saw me, I knew that she was going to be all right once she got her hormones balanced. The tears running down her face were now from laughter.

"At least if your raft tips over you won't

drown," she said. "You've got two floatation devices on your head!"

I looked so awful that the clinic receptionist called a nurse over to check on me instead of my friend.

"I'm fine," I insisted. "I brought in my friend. She's having a hormonal meltdown."

The nurse looked over at her.

"She looks perfectly fine compared to you," she said.

And she did. My girlfriend seemed to be cheering up by the minute. As I waited for her to get her blood drawn, every nurse, doctor, and patient that walked down the hall stopped to take a long look at me. The word on the street was "Marie is experiencing a horrible relapse of her postpartum depression. She looks *awful.*"

When we finally got back out to the car, my friend's dose of B vitamins, her hormone concoction injection in the tush, and her acupressure massage seemed to have kicked in fully. She appeared to be the picture of calm mental health. I, on the other hand, was exhausted from explaining to people that I was only having a reaction to tattoo dye. I didn't know which was worse: the look of sympathy for my assumed relapse into PPD, or the look of horror at my lapse in judgment in having my eyelids tattooed.

As I pulled back into the driveway, I looked at my swollen, oozing eyes in the rearview mirror. I was thinking: "I should have called my brother Wayne. He would have talked me out of having this done."

Wayne always thought I looked perfect no matter what. At this point in my life, I appreciate that more than I can possibly tell him. On my sixteenth birthday, though, his opinion made me want to disown him!

The day I turned sixteen, I was at the studio to tape the *Donny and Marie* show. I was waiting anxiously in my dressing room . . . not for the show to start, but for something much more life-changing: a complete earlobe transformation. The countdown to sixteen was over and I had arranged for a doctor to come and pierce my ears before we taped the show.

The scheduled time came and went. I couldn't understand why it wasn't happening. Then I found the cancellation culprit. Wayne. He was the one who had called off the appointment.

He pled his case to me, confessing that he couldn't imagine that his baby "Sissy" was ready for pierced ears. He told me, "You weren't born with holes in your ears, so you shouldn't be putting any in them."

I picked up my high heel and said to him,

"You weren't born with a hole in your head, either. But, if you don't get out of my dressing room, you'll be sporting a permanent Nine West shoe hat."

I was so upset I couldn't fathom making it through the day. I called my daddy, who was at home. Somehow he was able to understand various phrases through my sobbing: "you promised," "why did this happen?" and "canceled." My poor dad probably thought that the show had been canceled overnight.

He listened for about five minutes and then he stopped me.

Then he said, rather firmly, "Marie, you have to be a professional. People are counting on you right now to go out and do a show. There's a studio audience waiting, so dry your eyes."

I couldn't believe it! Didn't he understand how long I had waited for this day? Didn't I have every right to be upset? It was my birthday!

"Marie. Pull yourself together now. I'll be there in a little while," he told me.

I finally stopped sobbing and said, "Okay, Daddy."

I hung up the phone, dejected and a little angry. Then I looked at myself in the dressing room mirror. My face was splotchy from crying and my expression was that of a little child who didn't get her way. Even at sixteen, I was embarrassed for myself and my ridiculous hissy fit.

My father had not been heartless. He was only trying to teach me about priorities. My rite of passage into being a young woman wasn't prevented by my brother; it was only detoured. If I was mature enough to have my ears pierced, then I should be mature enough to deal with a temporary disappointment without dissolving into tears.

After the show, my father walked into my dressing room and said, "Marie, you're a big girl, now. I want to give you something and let you know that I trust you to make your own decisions."

My father placed in my hands a red velvet box. Inside were two perfect little diamond stud earrings. I cried again, but not from disappointment; they were tears of happiness that I had earned my father's trust. I still have the earrings and the little box.

My eyelids and my eyeliner tattoos looked normal in about a week, but not in time for the canoe trip. I told my daughter that we could tell everyone else that I fell face-first into a wasp's nest, even though I looked more like a fly.

Her suggestion was oversized, really dark sunglasses held in place with an elastic strap. I went with her suggestion . . . day and night! Not fun in the pitch-black when you're trying not to fall face-first in the woods!

My first three children are all old enough now to make their own decisions about things like tattoos. As my father did before me, I've tried to encourage them to wait and to make consequential decisions until they feel they are ready to live with their choices. The true rite of passage is in understanding the markings and piercings of life. Every day something can happen that punches a tiny hole into our sense of self. Each experience can put a permanent etch on our hearts. So you have to be patient until you can trust yourself to make the right decision.

THE MOST
CONSISTENT MAN

The safest place to be was always in my daddy's arms.
Osmond Family Archive

My father and I share a birthday: October 13. We also shared octopus stew, sparrow spit soup, and a delicacy that was described as warm monkey brains. I hoped it was only the name of the dish . . . like Gummi Worms aren't really worms . . . but it didn't stop either of us from giving it a try. I was an adventurous eater, like him, which gave us some special one on one time to spend together. If that meant swallowing jellyfish tentacles, well, then pass the tartar sauce.

My dad and I were big fans of sushi decades before it became popular in the United States. Raw fish wrapped in seaweed was always an option for the two of us as we explored various Asian cities from the 1960s through the 1980s. Not one of my brothers or my mother would ever join us on our mystery menu extravaganzas. They were all too chicken to try anything, except chicken. They missed out on a lot of good memories. Ironically, my father and I never got ill, but my brothers would brush their teeth using the local water and come down with a horrible case of Montezuma's revenge.

It wasn't hunger that motivated my father's search for the favorite local restaurant; it was his endless curiosity about people, which I know has been passed on to me. He was fascinated by how people lived and worked, not so much culturally as individually. The food was secondary to hearing about how the cook learned his craft, or seeing photos of the cashier's new baby, or discovering that the person sitting next to us at the counter was a stand-up comic. It didn't matter where we were in the world, my father could have a conversation with any person who made eye contact. Even with jet lag and exhaustion, my father would sit in the front seat of the cab and ask the driver about his life and goals. He knew the names of most of the crew at every venue, from the security guard to the spotlight operator.

In the last six months of his life, and three years after my mother had passed away, it became necessary for him, at age eighty-nine, to move to an assisted living residence because of a broken hip. One of my heroes, my oldest brother, Virl, had done everything possible to keep Daddy in his own home. Virl's own children were all grown, and he chose to become the anchor for both of our parents in their final years. Their firstborn child became their last day-to-day guardian, for which the rest of my brothers and I are all so grateful.

Of the thirty or more people living at this residence, my father was one of only three men. He had nonstop visitors from our huge family, and all of the nurses and other patients loved spending time with him.

One afternoon, he tapped on my arm and motioned with his eyes around the living room area.

"All of these women that live here are flirting with me," he whispered. "Do you think your mother would approve of that?"

"Well, you *are* quite a catch, Daddy," I said. "But you know, you might have misled them, asking them all about their lives. You're going to have to deal with it."

He chuckled, his blue eyes lighting up. "Sometimes they chase me down the hall," he whispered, "running with their walkers."

He wasn't kidding. More than once I would come in to find two women in their nineties bickering over who would get to sit next to George Osmond. One would be rubbing lotion into his "dry arms," and another would be trying to shove those arms into a sweater to "keep George warm."

My father was humble. He had spent time being a serviceman, a shoe salesman, a taxi driver, a builder, a postmaster, and he ran his own real estate business with my mother. And, of course, he managed our young careers. But no matter how my father made a living, he always "lived" for his family, and he taught us to have respect for every living thing, too.

Father bought a small ranch in Huntsville, Utah, when my brothers and I were very young. It was the place we longed to be anytime we weren't touring or taping shows in LA. It was the inspiration for my brothers' song "Down by the Lazy River," although we were never very lazy in Huntsville. As kids, we didn't know what it meant to be idle because we never saw either one of our parents just hang out.

My dad taught all of us kids to bait a hook, catch, clean, and cook fresh fish, ride a horse, round up cattle, use a bow and arrow, milk a cow, churn butter, plant a garden, harvest the garden, store fruit and vegetables, can them, and build a fire. And that was just in our first few months of life!

I think he knew it would be hard for us to get big heads if we were bent over picking sweet peas from the garden and then bowing our heads to say grace at a table full of food that we had grown. We understood the beginning of all good things.

Father appreciated the "fruits of his labor" and tried never to waste anything edible. As honorable as that is, sometimes the horn of plenty made us all squawk and try to skip breakfast. When we moved to Arleta, California, in the mid-1960s, Father was thrilled that citrus trees could be grown in our yard. One white grapefruit tree seemed to have full-grown fruit hanging from its branches year-round. It must have been some kind of freaky produce-aholic tree. My dad would pick huge grapefruits almost daily and, not to waste "the bounty of the earth," squeeze the juice so we each had a large glass waiting for us when we got up in the morning. I'm talking sixteen ounces of pure acid. Now, as an adult, it sounds refreshing, but as a little girl it was like pouring vinegar on your Frosted Flakes. (Sure, I'll try a side of rooster feet anytime, but daily pints of white grapefruit juice were another story.) At one point, Donny, Jay, and I devised a way to have some of the problem citrus "mysteriously disappear." We launched about fifty of the dreaded fruit over the fence and into the yard next door. They didn't vanish for long, as our irritated neighbor, dodging our blind throws, came to the fence to complain. She scolded us for littering her lawn and we quickly collected the bowling ball–sized fruit before our parents found out.

Playtime was always as full of energy as running the ranch, but that was the way my dad wanted us to view life: as an active adventure. He would get out our tents and we would camp and paddle canoes on the lake. We'd play touch football, softball, badminton, ride bikes, and hike. He taught us to shoot BB guns, and set up target practice for our bows and arrows. In the winter we would go tobogganing, ice fishing, and take hayrides around the ranch.

He also encouraged each of our separate interests, from Wayne getting his pilot's license as a teenager to Merrill's oil painting on velvet to Jimmy's passion for makeup prosthetics to Donny's obvious genius in electronics. (Yes, I tease him a lot, but Donny could wire stadium lights and the soundboard before the age of thirteen.) Even in his late eighties, my father still participated in anything he could learn, especially if it involved spending time with any of his kids. He sculpted a couple of dolls for my collectible doll line — including Georgette — which my mother named after him.

When my brothers and I were grown with our own kids, my father continued the adventures with every grandchild who came to stay. He taught them how to pull up onions and brand a calf. He let them drive the tractor with him and showed them how to catch night crawlers in the dampness of nightfall to use for fishing in the morning. He was always happiest in nature, working the earth, and celebrating the cycle of life. He even learned the ukelele so he could sing songs with his grandkids when they'd visit him in the nursing home.

It was never my father's intention that his young children become the family bread-winners. After all, he had always found a way to provide for his growing family. But we had this unusual and unique ability, the result of a beneficial mixture of DNA. He was repeatedly told that his children had a gift, not to be shuttered away, but to be shared with the world. How many young children are graced with perfect pitch and an ear for harmony starting when they first learn to talk? How many boys between the ages of five and eleven could sing four-part harmony together? They had a unique sound that has gone unrivaled among singing siblings to this day. When Jimmy was barely three years old he sang "Red Roses for a Blue Lady" perfectly, not only in English, but in Swedish and Japanese, too. Still, it was my grandfather, on my mother's side, who sent a tape recording of my brothers off to Hollywood.

When our careers were still fledgling and uncertain, my father had to risk leaving behind the business of real estate. We became his complete focus and he worked at it with all of his energy, which meant we worked very hard, too. We rehearsed, practiced, studied, and took every challenge to improve in the entertainment business. On live television there were no do-overs, so we practiced our act until Father felt that it was worthy of an audience of millions. From learning to ice skate to learning to tap dance, if we needed to take a crash course for an act in the next show, my dad found the best teacher available, and then ice skating or tap dancing became our constant until we had it down. My father was very wise with the money made by my brothers. He would first tithe ten percent in thanks to God for our many blessings. Then, he would invest half of the rest of the money into safe financial investments and the other half back into my brothers' careers for singing lessons, dance routines, and whatever else was needed to keep them armed with fresh, unique material, guaranteeing them a place for seven years on *The Andy Williams Show.*

The portfolio my father created was over the $100 million figure when he handed it over to my brothers in the late 80s. He felt at peace with a job well done as he and my mother went off to serve two different missions for our church: one year in Hawaii, and one year in London, England.

The "Made for TV" movies about our family portrayed my father as a controlling, angry stage parent.

In actuality, he was a man who did everything in his power to keep our family together in a business that is notorious for destroyed relationships.

In the short run, I think the sacrifice was about equal: we missed out on attending regular schools and the social aspects of being with other kids our age, and my father missed out by not having his own career advancements and a place of esteem in the eyes of his peers. He quietly faced harsh judgment from others for encouraging and supporting his children's entertainment careers. In the long run, the end results were not equal in the eyes of the world. My performing brothers and I each have vast portfolios including hit records, TV shows, and multiple other businesses and charities. My father ended his working years with the title of "Father Osmond." He wore it happily, which speaks volumes about his true humility.

Even as an adult, when I would go to visit my parents, they would have me join them in their bedroom for prayer.

They would look so cute with the covers pulled up to their chins. On the nightstands next to each side of the bed would be the ever-present foam heads, with my mother's wig attached to one and my father's hairpiece pinned to the top of the other. The foam heads were still decorated with the makeup Jimmy had applied to them when he was practicing for some scary Halloween getup. (Only later in life did my parents wear their natural hair, or lack thereof, in my dad's case. Fake hair was just easier. They were busy people.)

My parents would move to the edges of the bed and then pat the mattress between them.

"Come and be with us," my mom would say.

I'd climb between them, propping the pillow up against the headboard.

"Tell me all about everything you're doing," my dad would ask. As always, he was forever intrigued by life.

And we would talk until they started to snore — that was my cue to go. I'd turn out the lights and make my way to the spare bedroom.

One time, I took the kids to my parents' house for an overnight visit. As usual, late that night I found myself sitting on my parents' bed. My mother dozed off early, but I could tell my father had something on his mind.

In a rare moment between my father and me, tears spilled out of his eyes as he told me that he had been looking back at his life and his only worry was that he was too tough on my brothers and me.

I know that compared to the way other kids were raised, our lives were very out of the ordinary. He was strict, but there was never a question as to where we stood, which gave us great security. He had high expectations, but the rewards were higher for us. He made mistakes, but his faith in God always led him to act with integrity. He drew the line, but not around his heart. His heart was always open, full of love for my mother and for his children. He didn't always try to make everything all better for us; he gave us the skills to make it better for ourselves.

He and my mother raised eight great men. My father was the most consistent and honorable man I've known in my life.

When I would record my radio show in 2004, my father would come over to the studio and sit in to listen. He was so lonely for my mother after she passed away. I would always have a lunch ready to share with him — once in a while a plate of sushi.

He loved to listen on the headphones, to hear what people had to talk about when they called in. He would chuckle at the humor and get misty-eyed at the touching stories.

Usually after an hour or two, he'd move over to sit in the reclining chair so he could put his feet up and then he'd take a nap. Sometimes people would call in and ask, "Is that someone snoring in the background?" Yes. It was. I loved it that my father could finally just hang out. And I prayed that he could rest easy in a job well done.

Boogie Woogie
Twenty Miles in
Fifteen Minutes
Flat

"Our scheduled on-time arrival for Christmas day was delayed due to unexpected turbulence"

Happy Holidays & best wishes for 2009

Donny & Marie

from Marie and Stephen, Jessica, Rachael, Michael, Brandon, Brianna, Matthew, and Abigail. Also, Lola and Baby

I was even late sending out Christmas cards, so this was a post–New Year's delivery.

Photo by: Kim Goodwin

My dad taught my brother Alan to play the bugle as a boy. It was then Alan's chore to wake us up almost every morning with reveille. Since my dad was an army sergeant who was later constantly jostled about by the unpredictable life of show business and nine kids, I think that certain elements of daily routine were his way of staying sane. Waking up to the blast of a brass instrument cannot be described as pleasant, but I sometimes wish I still had that option instead of my alarm clock. After all, it's impossible to throw a young man playing a bugle across the room without getting out of bed. When Father was in charge, I was always on time, to everything.

Left to my own devices, I tend to run a little bit late. I'm eternally hurried. It seems no matter how early I start to get ready, I still find myself scrambling to get out the door.

Donny would say, and has said, that I am always running late, but I like to call it living in the moment. I admit, sometimes my "moments" gel together to become thirty minutes or more, but as they say, time flies when you're having fun, so I must be a joy-loving person. How's that for female logic?

Donny is exactly like my father when it comes to minding the minute hand.

You would have to search far and wide to find anyone who was ever miffed that Donny arrived late. It doesn't happen, unless he's drugged. In forty-five years of professional appearances, so far, that has only happened once.

A couple of weeks before the opening of the *Donny and Marie* show at the Flamingo Hotel in Las Vegas, Donny and I made an appearance on *Good Morning America* on the outdoor stage in New York City's Bryant Park. *Good Morning America* actually starts live programming in the middle of the night. Well, at least it feels that way if you are traveling from West Coast time for an East Coast performance. Our plane had landed at around ten p.m. at the John F. Kennedy Airport, just in time to get a few hours of sleep and be on the set at four thirty a.m. The Osmonds may not have powers to time travel, but we can definitely time-zone travel. We are pretty used to losing three hours, then gaining ten, going forward a day, then back eight hours all in the name of an international tour. Most people would find it a challenge to fall asleep at eleven p.m. when their body is telling them that it's barely dinnertime. Personally, I'm used to being able to sleep soundly whenever the chance arises: sitting on a crate of anvils backstage with my head resting against the wall, leaning against an airplane window, having my roots touched up by a colorist, in a dental chair while having a root canal, or even with wet painted fingernails propped up on pillows and one or two kids with restless limb syndrome flailing about my bed like electric eels. Give me only sixty seconds and I can go unconscious. I mean willingly! I can also go unwillingly unconscious on live television in about one second, but that's another story, or millions of views on YouTube.

The following morning I arrived on the *Good Morning America* set, only a handful of minutes late (okay, twenty-three), surprised to hear producers ask me: "Where's Donny?" They seemed truly concerned. I was sure he must have arrived ahead of me. He always does. I shrugged it off, assuming he was in the lighting booth designing a special effect on the computer or rewiring the electric keyboards, which he can do in his sleep. Little did I know that he *was* in his sleep when he showed up with only minutes to spare before we were to go on the air. His face was pale and kind of mushed up and his eyes were glazed over. That was really a twist because it's usually my eyes that glaze over when he's talking to me about electronics.

We performed three times that morning, one set in each half hour of *Good Morning America,* to more than a thousand people gathered in the park. We had rehearsed each number before we performed it for the show, but as soon as the cameras rolled, Donny was not doing one thing that we had rehearsed. Though it shocked me, I thought it was pretty fun and spontaneous for Mr. Punctual!

For the most part, it all went off without a hitch, but following the show on the way to the airport, Donny told me that he had absolutely no memory of the past two hours.

Then I found out why. He had been putting in long, intense hours every day producing and editing the videos for our Vegas show.

He was anxious about being alert and

ready for the early-morning performance, so after we had checked in to the hotel the previous night, he decided to take a sleep aid, one he had carried around in his travel bag for years and had never used. One of the side effects, though rare, is temporary amnesia.

It's probably a good thing we are Mormon and don't drink or do drugs, because our chemical tolerance is ridiculously low. Balsamic vinaigrette and antihistamine nasal spray can make us giddy, I swear.

He asked me if it all went well. I told him yes even though I'm sure at some point he'll probably see a replay of his attempt to apply the Heimlich maneuver to Diane Sawyer for no apparent reason. He may never look it up on YouTube, but I'm keeping a copy to use for ammunition someday when my unavoidable tardiness sends him over the edge. Working with someone as punctual as Donny, it's good to have one ace up your sleeve to be able to say: "Remember when . . . ??"

I'm not trying to excuse my habit of running behind, but please, the playing field is so uneven when it comes to the amount of time a woman needs to get ready compared to what men need. If the most complicated part of getting ready for me was to adjust a slipknot on a necktie, I like to think I'd be twenty minutes early to everything.

Most women I know have this list of activities to complete before finding the car keys to leave: curling or flat-ironing hair; pressing out the wrinkles on your face, creaming it up, swabbing it down, spatulaing, sponging, spraying, powder puffing; using wands, tubes, glue and tweezers, nylon, elastic, underwires, and control topping; as well as plucking, shaping, outlining, bronzing, and then blending it all together. Brush hair and then lint roll the runaways; hook, zip, and stretch; coordinate the metalware: earrings, watch, bracelets, necklace, and a hair bobble or two. Then . . . you have to find something to really wear once you realize the outfit you originally picked out looks ridiculous. Find two shoes that are the same style and color. (I don't know about you, but sometimes I need a flashlight to do this step.) Now you might be ready to go unless you have to change out purses, which adds another five to seven minutes.

Then a woman usually has to repeat at least five of the above steps with and for any person in the household under age eighteen.

Here's the male checklist: splash water on face, apply one dab of hair gel, find two matching shoes (and not even heels! I might add), make sure fly is up, put wallet in back pocket, grab the car keys, and . . . go.

Still, when Donny and I decided to do this show together at the Flamingo, I made a silent vow to myself that I was not going to be late. I figured I had lost forty-six pounds of weight in less than a year, now it was time to lose my habit of losing track of time.

The first week of our six-month run, I was feeling pretty good about my resolution. I was on time to almost every rehearsal, was ready to go for almost every press occasion and meeting, and . . . so far . . . had arrived for each of the four shows in plenty of time. And, to top it all off, it was the same week I had enrolled the four younger kids in their school, bought and organized school outfits, supplies, sports and scouting equipment, and schedules for the month. My seventeen-year-old, Michael, had been accepted into a performing arts program for high school students. He's always had an incredible musical ear and the ability to pick up almost any instrument and play it, in the same way his grandpa did.

When Saturday arrived, I took my four little kids, along with Michael, and drove to a nearby health food emporium to pick out some nutritious snacks and dinner food for our family time. Since I have lost weight by eating better, my kids have become more conscious of their own choices. After seeing the massive salad bar, they asked if they could fix to-go cartons for an early dinner. As I helped Abby pick out some carrot sticks and sliced beets, I answered Matthew and Brandon's repeated questions of "What's that???" as they pointed to bins of tofu and creamed eggplant.

Then I saw the edamame (soy beans in the pod), which is Rachael's favorite, so I said to Michael, "Maybe we should make a salad to take home to Rachael."

"No, Mom," Mike answered. "She's not at home. She's at work."

"Okay," I said, checking out the spicy hummus dip.

That was when a cold reality washed over me, as if someone had turned on the sprinkler system to hose off the produce.

"Rachael's at work???" I screeched, scaring the kids into a fast freeze.

The reason for my panic was that Rachael works with me, as my wardrobe assistant for the Flamingo show. If Rachael was at work, there was a 100 percent chance that I should be there, too.

I looked down at my watch. It was only three thirty-five p.m., hours before the seven thirty show. But what I had failed to remember was that every Saturday in September, we did two shows. The first one was a four p.m. matinee! What's worse was that the Flamingo Hotel was no less than twenty miles west of my current location. That would mean a twenty-five-minute drive without any traffic tie-up at all.

"Drop your tongs!" I barked at the kids. "Grab your containers and . . . run!"

Getting through the checkout line was a complete blur, but I'm pretty sure I tipped the cashier 120 percent of the bill as I couldn't even wait for the change. As we dashed across the parking lot, I kept a fast hold on Abby's hand so she couldn't slow to a walk from a jog.

"My mini corns!" Abby cried out, as tiny pickled corncobs bounced out of her open container and torpedoed to the asphalt below.

"Mommy's sorry, sweetheart," I said to calm her dismay. "I'll get you some more for Christmas." Lucky for me, guarantees like this tend to make sense to six-year-olds.

I had left my cell phone plugged into the car to recharge. Not surprisingly I had about fourteen missed calls and a long list of text messages all saying the same thing: "Where are you????"

I checked in the rearview mirror to make sure every kid and every limb was inside the car and then I backed out of the parking space, pressing the speed dial to my manager, Karl, on my cell phone.

He answered: "Marie! Where are you?"

I've never understood why people want to know your geographical location when it's obvious you're not where you're supposed to be.

"I've decided I can't take it anymore and I'm driving up the coast of California," I said, because self-deprecation is my best defense when I've put myself in a bind.

Karl responded, "Matthew is nine years old. I'm sure you don't have postpartum depression anymore."

I had to laugh. "Karl, trust me. I'm on my way to the theater, but I'm really late."

"Well, there's a sold-out house full of people here, looking forward to seeing the show," Karl said. "So hurry."

There's nothing like a dose of guilt peppered onto panic to make you feel like it's all going to turn out all right. But somehow I knew it would. I took a moment to say a silent prayer for safety and calmness. As always, the result was a feeling of being graced with a sense of peace.

For some reason, the cars in the lanes

ahead of me moved aside like floating icebergs, parting to let the "mothership" pass. The kids were quiet and my mind began to process what I needed to do to be ready for the show.

Karl rang my phone again. "Should I tell the stage manager that we need to hold the show?"

"No! No," I said. "Just give Donny a sleeping pill. I'll be there."

I pulled into the Flamingo parking garage fifteen minutes later. (Maybe we *can* time travel!) As I shifted into park, Michael said to me: "Run ahead, Mom. I'll bring the kids."

At the top of the elevator, my daughter Rachael grabbed my arm and dashed me into my dressing room. It was five minutes before four o'clock. She and my makeup person, Kim, had laid out my costume across the floor so I could literally walk into it all.

Kim yanked a brush with hairspray on it through my hair to smooth it down as Rachael taped my audio cords to my neck. Someone dropped to the floor, shoving my feet into my show shoes, then tugged out the earrings I was wearing and replaced them with the show jewelry.

There was no time for makeup, so I

resorted to my Sharpie marker, which can be used as eyeliner, mascara, and to mark my beauty dot near my eye. From years of lateness, I've learned exactly what lines to draw on my face to give me the appearance of being in complete makeup. I threw on a layer of lipstick as the stage manager came through the door.

"Places!" she called out. She looked a bit surprised. "Are you really ready?"

"Ready!" I said, turning to greet her with a smile. I knew that up close, I probably looked a bit like a send-up of Carol Burnett playing Gloria Swanson playing Norma Desmond in *Sunset Boulevard,* but I was hoping that with the stage lights no one would notice my crooked lip line and smudged eyeliner corners.

I turned to mouth the words "Thank you!" to my dressing assistants as I exited behind the stage manager. Their quick thinking saved my backside . . . and my front side, too.

At the beginning of every show, Donny and I descend a flight of metallic stairs, side by side, singing our opening number, but first a set of powerful lights shadows our image in silhouette on the white scrims that hang between us and the audience.

As the preshow music started up, I joined

Donny at the top of the staircase to strike our usual pose. It was exactly four p.m.

Donny looked over at me and squinted his eyes suspiciously. He could tell that there was something not quite right, but he wouldn't be able to say that I was late. About halfway through the show I sing a tribute to my mother and father, their favorite song, "Boogie Woogie Bugle Boy." I think it was one of my best performances ever of that song. I was swinging those lyrics. I guess it could be the "clap your hands and stomp your feet" rhythm of it, but I'm pretty sure it was the jolts of natural adrenaline that were still pumping through my veins from my close call with missing the matinee. It really is a good thing that Osmonds don't drink or do drugs, because I was flying high for the whole show and through the evening performance, too. By the way, I didn't dare leave the theater between shows. I wasn't about to push my luck!

"Wise Men Say"

A doll and a good laugh were always my MO.
Osmond Family Archive

The most phenomenal bouquets of flowers that were ever sent to our hotel while we worked in Vegas weren't for me. They weren't for Donny, either, or any of my brothers, for that matter. They were for my mother. They were from Elvis Presley.

Elvis Presley adored my mother. He met her after one of my brothers' early Las Vegas appearances. He looked closely at my mother's face and then stopped to talk to her for quite a while. My brothers and I stood by, watching in awe, as my mother began a lifelong friendship with him. Now, both Elvis Presley and the Queen of England had my mother's phone number!

Pictures of Elvis's own mother, Gladys, show a resemblance to my mother. Both of them had dark wavy hair, a round, soft face, and lively eyes. Elvis had lost his mother in 1958 (she was only forty-six), and he never got over missing her. I understand that now.

My mother could always sense when some-one needed a mom no matter who they were, how old they were, or how thick their pork chop sideburns grew in! Elvis Presley became one of millions of people from around the world who called my mother "Mother Osmond."

Often I would see her, late in the night at the kitchen table, or while waiting in an airport, handwriting a letter to one of our fans, someone she had never met. She cared about them all. As I watched her, I learned what it meant to be a truly loving presence in the lives of others.

In July of 2008, after Donny and I performed at the MGM in Las Vegas, a woman who was waiting outside the stage door handed me a letter, handwritten by my mother more than thirty years before. Though she had never met my mother in person, she told me of getting the letter in the mail as a fifteen-year-old girl, and how my mom's words had given her hope in the midst of a horrible family situation. She wanted to return it to me, knowing how much I missed my mother. The letter was full of comforting words and positive think-ing mantras for the young girl to tell herself. In addition to her amazing capacity to love, my mother was also way ahead of her time.

She was ecstatic with the invention and growing popularity of e-mail, and she told me that she couldn't wait for the day she could strap a rocket pack to her waist and zoom off to visit family and friends living on Mars.

Every month she wrote a "Mother Osmond Memo" (M.O.M.) to catch up family and friends on everything from our latest news to how well her sweet peas were growing in the garden. She would include good time-saving tips she had heard about, memorable quotes, organizational skills, and recipes. What began as a letter mailed to about fifty people grew to reach thousands of fans around the world by e-mail. She always wrote in the same heartfelt style, as if it continued to be read only by her loved ones. She would end some of her letters by writing, "I'd like to hear from all of you — would like to know who's out there!!" She'd sign off with "Sing-cerely, Mother Osmond." She would hear from them, thousands of replies, people writing back, updating my mother on their lives, attaching photos of their weddings, pets, and then kids. She would respond to as many as she could, especially to those who wrote to her of any heartache they were going through. Just as she had responded to Elvis Presley's heartache as a son missing his mother and his humble need for motherly advice about his loneliness as a iconic superstar. She always seemed glad to hear from Elvis when he would call her to check in. He would ask my mother her thoughts and opinions on choices he was making in his career and even his personal life. He trusted my mother to keep his privacy. He had great intuition that way. He couldn't have picked a better person. She never shared with us anything personal he would tell her. Though he passed away thirty years before my mom, she still took his confidences to her grave.

Even as a little girl, I understood how famous Elvis really was, and when I heard my mother talking to him on the phone, I would find any excuse to be in the same room. After a few moments she would shoo me out of earshot, but I would still try to listen from the next room to my mother's counsel to him. Come on! It was Elvis!

She was always ready with some kind words, encouraging him like she did each of us, to pray for answers and read the scriptures.

Elvis, in return, gave us some life-changing show business advice.

One afternoon in Las Vegas, at the International Hotel, where Elvis was performing, he sat my family down and suggested a costume change for my brothers. He thought they should all wear sequined jumpsuits onstage, much like his own. Before this time no one wore a jumpsuit, except paratroopers!

Considering the success that Elvis was having with his brand-new look, my family jumped on the idea. The "barbershop" matching blazers and straw Kellies look went out and matching bell-bottom jumpsuits came in. Just as it had for Elvis, it was a look that defined the Osmonds. (I had a couple of mind-boggling jumpsuits that I sported myself in the midseventies. One was khaki colored and another an impractical cream color. They were both so tight that every time I bent over the snaps would pop open. Thankfully, that trend didn't last long for women. You had to completely disrobe to use a restroom. Who has time for that? No, thanks.)

"Make sure your kids always stay close to their fans" was the more experienced advice Elvis gave to my mother. He had regrets about following a suggestion to remain aloof. He told her that it had been a struggle for him to be himself on a day-to-day basis, because the fans didn't really know him or accept him as a real person.

Elvis always felt a deep responsibility to entertain his fans, to make sure they left happy. My parents respected that about Elvis, and they encouraged us to apply a similar principle to our young lives.

My brothers and I weren't raised to be celebrities. We were groomed to be entertainers — to make people happy. I was less than two years old when my brothers performed at Disneyland and were offered a contract on the Disneyland summer stage. Alan was twelve, and Jay was only six. I never knew a day of my childhood life where music wasn't being played, practiced, written, or sung. Even on Sundays, we sang together as a family in church. Until I was about five years old, I had mistakenly concluded that every family must do the same thing we did: perform. This misconception was reinforced by the fact that our close family friends were, and still are, the famous Lennon Sisters. They are four sisters who appeared weekly on *The Lawrence Welk Show* for thirteen years. They were just like us. They wore matching outfits. They sang harmonies. They toured with Andy Williams. We were so busy, I obviously had no idea what type of lives other children led.

My brothers' early career was similar to the path Elvis had been through in the mid-fifties, performing one local show at a time, city to city, venue to venue. There was no such thing as an *American Idol* road to fame or to a record contract in eight weeks.

The Osmond Brothers' first tour bus was a used Greyhound. Not a refurbished Greyhound, just a used one. There were no couches or kitchenette, no microwaves or DVD players. It was only bus seats and an aisle and a closed-in toilet at the back. My family rode in the front half of the bus, and our band took over the back half. Now I understand why my mother always wore wigs in the late 1960s and early 1970s. She always had to stick her head out the window to catch a breath of fresh air! Then when we arrived at the next venue, she'd plop the wig back on to look good.

Donny, Jimmy, and I made little bunks by throwing blankets and pillows on the aluminum luggage racks above the seats and crawling up there for a nap. We practiced our songs from town to town and always did our lessons. Mother would walk up and down the aisle of the bus, checking our schoolwork, listening to us read out loud. This was the way we traveled, from show to show, from the Elks lodges to the county fairs to the outdoor festivals. As a family, we loaded and unloaded our own instruments, costumes, and microphones. We would set up on whatever stage was made available, using whatever amplification system was there, and play to the audience that had gathered.

My mother and I counted the unsold tickets, called "deadwood," to help determine ticket sales for each show. I would walk into the box office with my mom and the personnel would say: "I've heard of you. The only sister, right? You've become famous across the country as the 'ticket terror.' "

Yes. Before I found my passion to perform, I found it first in being the only one who could find the one missing ticket number in a bundle of five hundred.

The first couple of years doing shows in Las Vegas, our home base was an Airstream trailer my father had hitched to the car. We would get one hotel room and take turns using the shower. We would also take turns staying in the room so we could sleep in a real bed. My mother would buy sandwich bread and cold cuts (usually olive loaf — I guess she thought since her name was on it, she should buy it) and make lunches on the tiny countertop in the Airstream. Every night after the shows, we would gather in the trailer for our family time, learn the stories of the Bible, and then pray. With nine growing kids and two adults, we would squeeze around the little table, scrunch up cross-legged on the beds, perch on the steps, and even hang out of the bathroom door. (Want to play Barrel of Monkeys, anyone?)

Why we crowded into the Airstream and not the hotel room was somehow never questioned. But as long as we were crammed into the trailer, closeness was unavoidable, and for my parents, I think that was the point. For all of the successes that were to come, the hardships of those years hold the best memories for me. Even when the income from performing increased, my parents still chose humble accommodations. My father, especially, wanted to be certain that we never put ourselves above anyone else. After almost every show, my brothers and I would stand, greet our fans, and sign hundreds of autographs.

One time, on the edge of my teen years, we were doing a summertime show at a state fair. It was miserably hot, and following the show I grumbled at the thought of having to stand in line, shake hands, and take pictures for another hour.

My mother said to me, "Marie, many of these fans looked forward to this day for a long time. This might be the most fun they will have all year because their lives are so hard. Some of them probably had to save their money for months and months to come and see you. It's only one more hour in your life, but it's a lifelong memory for them."

Okay. Fine! If you put it *that* way!!!

Honestly, I'm so grateful that she put it that way. Because of my parents, and perhaps first because of Elvis Presley, my brothers and I have had fans that are like our family. They are the ones responsible for giving my brothers and me such long careers. Elvis was a wise man.

When I was on season five of *Dancing with the Stars,* the producers told me that my fans jammed the phone lines voting for me. They sent bags full of letters to the show and thousands of e-mails to my Web site. Many longtime fans wrote to me of their support, but thousands of new fans, some as young as ten, also wrote to me with encouragement and a thank-you for helping them feel like it's possible to take on a challenge. Every day, when I would drag my aching body to another dance rehearsal, I would think of them. I pushed myself because they made me happy and I wanted to give it my all because of their hopes in me.

When we danced the Viennese waltz to Elvis Presley's "Can't Help Falling in Love," my partner, Jonathan Roberts, choreographed a move where I did a death-drop spin on the floor. After fifteen hours of rehearsal, I had a huge bruise on my hip, and it started to take on various shapes and colors. By the day of the show, I noticed something about my growing bruise that made me stop in my tracks. I have heard all the various stories of people seeing an image of the Virgin Mary in things like a piece of toast, but there, on the side of my leg, life-sized, was the unmistakable profile of Elvis Presley. What an appropriate time for him to show up. Not that much has changed in thirty years. Here I was in a cramped trailer, in the parking lot of the CBS studios, in the blazing heat of a Los Angeles afternoon, going over performance notes. There was a knock at my door. It was my sweet brothers, who had come to watch the show.

THE FRILL IS GONE

Me at three . . .
Osmond Family Archive

. . . and my youngest daughter, Abigail, at three. Is poofy learned or inherited?
Osmond Family Archive

A soldier, a ballerina, a major league baseball player, and a political campaigner: these are the people I've been meeting. Not one of them has had one good word to say. In fact, the ballerina even spit at me. Or maybe I should say spit up *on* me. I guess they'll all talk soon enough, once they have language skills. They're all babies, under a year old, though their outfits make them look like they should carry business cards.

I've seen newborn boys dressed like they are ready to conduct a symphony, complete with a little black jacket, white shirt and bow tie, and baby girls accessorized with a designer purse before they could hold a spoon. I drove by a day-care play lot and it looked like a job fair! Ever seen a plump toddler toddling along in pumps and a pencil skirt?

I love babies: squishy, mushy, delicate, innocent babies. It's perplexing why we dress an infant in camouflage or sports jerseys or mini-tuxedos. I mean, in the big life picture, it's only a matter of months that we even get to dress our children like a baby and win over the hearts of every person in a room without even trying. Why rush it? I think we should help our babies play that card as long as possible.

I cherished every second of pink and pale blue with my own eight little cherubs. I pre-selected the outfits they wore home from the hospital with almost as much care as I chose their names. I have stored away those debut tiny gowns for them to keep, the delicate embroidered rosebuds, the cashmere bunting, the irresistible ivory buttons. And even though my teenagers have openly mocked my sentimentality, whenever I bring the coming-home gowns out of storage, they are still beguiled by what small creatures they once were.

It's pure joy for me to shop for white frilly booties and tiny knit sweaters, scrumptious sleepers and sweet little receiving blankets, all featuring nothing more mature than a newly hatched duckling. Babies don't need sophisticated clothes to make a first impression. If you're little enough to wear a onesie, then your statement is: "Hey, look at me! I'm brand-new!"

My lifelong friend Patty, who has been present, by my side, through the first days of life for every one of my kids, is a witness to my baby-dressing zeal. She claims that I put so many ruffles on my baby girls that their arms stuck straight out like wings on a pastel-colored 747.

It's true. They did resemble tiny, yummy pastries for the first two years. I had the same experience when I was a little girl with the way my mother dressed me. I don't think my hands touched my sides until I was nine. I have film footage of me, at age two, on Christmas Day. My parents had given me a child-sized rocking chair. As excited as I was to sit in it, the layers and layers of my petticoats couldn't fit between the armrests. The rocking chair disappeared completely, engulfed by crinoline. I was their only daughter and my free will in the fashion area was overridden by my parents' desperate need for a touch of the feminine among all their boys. Can you blame them?

Keeping with tradition, I decided that until my babies learned to say the word "no," they were mine to dress up in darling blue rompers and white knee socks, even before their kneecaps came into existence. (Interesting baby fact: We are born without kneecaps and develop them between ages two and six.) The only mock-adult accessories they wore were sailor caps. And, like many moms, I've put an elastic pink ribbon headband on my girls before they had seven strands of caterpillar silk hair to hold into place. For special occasions, I even hot glued silk flowers to the handles of their binkies. I was wise enough to photograph these adorable moments, because they didn't last nearly long enough.

My kids each displayed their fashion free will pretty early on. Like most children, mine began inching toward independence by dressing exactly the opposite of how I dressed them as babies. Even as toddlers, my children sent me the message loud and clear. Soft baby blue corduroy overalls were all over by age three, replaced by track pants and SpongeBob T-shirts. Floral sundresses with smocking were given the smack down and replaced by distressed jeans and polar fleece vests.

My first daughter, at age five, made a fashion statement that left me speechless, mostly because I was laughing. I opened the front door to find her riding a big-wheeled trike up and down the driveway, wearing only black leggings, snow boots, and her brother's six-foot rubber play snake like a choker around her neck. It was clear to me that I needed to back off the Laura Ashley look or I was going to have a Hells Angel for a kid.

From then on, I may have made fashion suggestions, but, within reason, my children always made their own fashion choices. Growing up on TV and having to wear hundreds of different costumes, I completely understand the issue of the outer appearance not matching the inner self. As a teenager, on our variety show, I was dressed up as everything from a chimney sweep to a cheerleader, from a goatherd to an Egyptian queen, from Princess Leia in *Star Wars* to a vaudeville flapper. It was complicated to be a fifteen-year-old girl trying to figure out who I was, especially when I was dressed as Mae West. "Why don't you come up and be me sometime?"

In an ironic twist, as twists usually are, my youngest daughter, the last in the line, can't seem to get enough of the überfeminine. With her as a toddler and me as a tired middle-aged mommy, I was ready to move us both into the more practical world of cotton stretch pants and zip-up hoodies. She was having none of it. She would scowl at a sneaker and turn away from a T-shirt. Most girls start going through the schizophrenic daily process of clothing selection that involves ten or more trial outfits at around age sixteen; my little one started at age five.

Getting her out the door to school is a challenge as we navigate through a pile of the frilly and the pink, the hair bobbles and the bows, the ballerina shoes in every color. And just like her mother, she never leaves the house without a lip gloss in her purse.

Now, when I'm the first one in my night-gown every night and can't wait to scrub the makeup off my face, she wants to put on her Arabelle gown with jeweled tiara and give each other glittery manicures.

It serves me right.

FIGHT OR FLEE

I hated my dress, my hair, my gut, sitting up straight, and obviously posing in a ladylike fashion with my knees together. Whoops!

Osmond Family Archive

179

I sometimes wonder what ever happened to the girdle I rescued from the San Fernando earthquake. I guess it didn't have quite the importance I gave it back in 1971, because it's long gone. I wish I still had one or two of the miniature glass animal figurines I had collected from around the world at that time, but they broke because I couldn't grab them. My hands were full. After all, I had a tummy panel sewn into Lycra to save.

When it comes to "fight or flee" situations and the answer is flee, I'm always fascinated to see what people take with them. When the Malibu fires were spreading rapidly across the hills in the fall of 2007, I watched the TV interviews of people packing their cars, preparing to abandon their homes. It wasn't what they were saying that I found compelling, it was what they were saving. Men seemed to be loading up their electronics, golf clubs, and other things made of metal. Women dashed from the house to the car with stacks of photo albums, handmade quilts, kid necessities, and armloads of clothes on hangers. Everyone packed up the pets, but I didn't see one plant.

If I had been at home when my own house caught on fire in 2005, I'd like to imagine that I would have acted the same way after I knew my family was safe: get the sentimental and irreplaceable belongings. I have reason to believe, however, that I'd be just like a woman I met in Chicago. She told me that when the fire alarm went off in her high-rise apartment building, she found herself standing on the sidewalk five minutes later "with a rolling suitcase full of cosmetics." As she explained, "If I was going to have to live in a shelter, at the very least I wanted to look good." Hey, I understand that completely! When traveling by plane, I always carry on my makeup. I think airline security hates me. Sorry, but if your luggage is lost, you can get away with wearing the same outfit twice, but two-day-old makeup always looks like . . . well, two-day-old makeup.

Being in show business, the pressure to always look good had sadly been ingrained in me so deeply by age ten that even an earthquake couldn't shake that concern from my head. I was too worried about my tummy shaking. I felt like I had a lot to live up to and a lot to lose, literally.

I guess by the time my mother was pregnant with me, all of the DNA containing long eyelashes, slender body type, strong straight teeth, and thick wavy hair had been used up by my seven older brothers. As my mother's only girl, I was blessed with the leftover goods in the genes department: tiny eyelashes and a propensity toward belly blubber. I was pretty unhappy being that chubby little girl with greasy bangs and a mouth full of cavity-prone teeth, including one that had grown in like a fang. It got me teased for being an "uncommitted vampire."

I now know that some of my weight issues were in reaction to difficult issues of my childhood, which I wrote about in *Behind the Smile.* I dreaded being on the cover of *Tiger Beat* magazine along with my brothers. I wanted to hide in the background as much as I could. I must have thought that wearing a girdle would hold me together in all the ways I felt flawed in this family of what seemed like perfect boys.

There are almost no photos of me from ages eight to eleven, because one summer evening I gathered them all up and tossed them into the barbecue in the backyard.

They made for some pretty tasty roasted marshmallows that night, though no one else was aware of the reason why. I wasn't worried about frying my eyelashes near the flames; I didn't have any to lose.

We had taped an *Andy Williams Christmas Special* only months before, where we all wore holiday attire, complete with fake fur hats and scarves and winter parkas. Nothing makes a girl feel more like a formless blob than a parka!

Even though I was very shy, I was part of the family, and Andy wanted everyone to be onstage with him. I don't remember the choreography, the song we sang, or much at all about that show. My only memory is of overhearing two producers talking in the hallway: "How do we get the fat sister out of the camera shot?" one asked the other.

My closet at home was shaped like a wedge, wide at the front where the rods hung across. The back side of the closet came to a point that was out of sight unless you looked under the hanging clothing. It was my retreat. That night, I crawled into the back corner and, drawing my knees up toward my chin, buried my face in my hands. I choked back as much of my sobbing as I could, hoping that my brothers and parents could not hear me. I wished I could disappear. I wanted to start over again, to be born beautiful like Donny.

Little did I know that it was only the beginning of thirty years of complicated issues regarding my body image.

For about a decade my mother had a wringer washer that she refused to give up, even though they were horribly outdated. She liked to line dry the clothes and only a wringer truly squeezed all the water out, better than the spin cycle on any washing machine. I used to help by taking the clothes, post-squeezing, and putting them into a basket. I would stand there and daydream: "Wouldn't it be cool if I could put my tummy through that wringer and, 'poof' . . . or maybe I should say 'pop,' be as thin as my older brothers?" They seemed to be able to eat whatever they wanted, whenever they wanted, and never had to think about being able to get their shirts buttoned up.

As a family treat, my father would buy huge boxes of Fudgsicles at a local drive-thru dairy. He would stock the freezer full. There were so many of us that my parents would buy all food products in bulk. Unfortunately, I was the only one who bulked up!

My dad would try to motivate me by saying that I could have some when I lost a pound or two. That only motivated me to get clever in the sneaking-a-snack department. I would stay awake into the night until I heard my brothers go to bed and my parents snoring. That was a sure signal that the coast was finally clear. Then I would creep silently downstairs into the kitchen and take two Fudgsicles (or six or seven) back up to my bedroom to enjoy them in privacy. I hid the evidence of the wooden sticks under my mattress. This worked well until the day my parents went to replace my bed and several hundred Fudgsicle sticks fell to the floor.

They called me into my room, where my mother was pointing at them, scattered across the floor. I looked up, into their faces, and said the first thing I could think of to break the tension.

"Arts-and-crafts projects, anyone?"

I don't remember how I became the owner of my first girdle by age ten, but my mother most likely saw my distress at feeling chubby and found the most practical solution. After all, in that era women didn't really do sit-ups or concern themselves with muscle tone: it was all about the foundation undergarments. They wore girdles! I mean, they had to wash and wax the floors. Why in the world would they even think about doing sixty sit-ups?

The San Fernando earthquake struck in the early-morning hours. Our house, in Arleta, California, became a lot more rock 'n' roll than Donny could ever hope to be. The evening before, at ten p.m., when the female Osmonds always get their "second wind," my mother had very impulsively decided to switch around the order of the kitchen. She and I stayed up quite late moving the glassware from the open shelves into the cupboards and the canned goods to where the glassware had been. It was good intuition because, making our way through the kitchen during the aftershocks, we only had to dodge rolling cans instead of splintered glass.

Our Airstream trailer was parked in our backyard, and Alan and Wayne and Merrill were sleeping in it that night. They called it their bachelor pad because it gave them space outside of the house. During the earthquake, Wayne said, he thought someone had hooked the trailer onto a car and was driving them down the freeway at eighty miles per hour.

Jay's prized possession, a giant Buddha sculpted from metal that had been given to him by a Japanese fan, plummeted off the wall above his bed and landed directly on his pillow moments after he sat up. I screamed and rolled out of my own bed, my head landing in the wastebasket. Bookcases toppled over and lamps crashed to the floor. The earthquake was so intense, it shook most of the water out of our swimming pool, leaving the lawn flattened down, as if it had gone through Mother's wringer.

When the whole family finally gathered in the front yard, shivering in our pajamas, I looked down to see what was in my hands. In my panic to get to safety, not knowing if the house was going to collapse on our heads, I had grabbed my girdle as something I couldn't live without. In my other hand was my set of Klackers, a popular toy that year. They were two hard acrylic globes at either end of a folded string. The object was to "klack" them together above and then below your hand as fast as you could. They were soon taken off the market because of the injuries they caused children. Klackers could crack a skull pretty easily. If my brothers ever felt like laughing at my unreasonable choice of what to save, they never did in front of me. Perhaps it was because of the Klackers.

By age sixteen I had learned to live with being hungry quite often in order to stay slender. I was five feet five and weighed only 110 pounds, when a producer of the *Donny and Marie* show made it absolutely clear to me that unless I lost ten pounds to look better on camera, the entire show would be canceled and scores of people would be out of work, all because — as he put it — I couldn't keep food out of my mouth.

I figured out how to keep almost all food out of my mouth pretty quickly. As good as I was at sneaking Fudgsicles at age ten, I was even better at hiding that I was eating nothing at all on most days. I would tell my mother that I had eaten breakfast before she got up and then wave off any offers of dinner saying that I had already eaten at the studio before I came home. I would drink lemon squeezed into water with maple syrup and cayenne pepper all day long for four days out of the week. The weekends were the only time I would let myself eat real food, but not without some horrible guilt that it would all show up by Monday on my stomach. When I got down to ninety-three pounds, I still didn't feel I was thin enough — even when I became too weak from hunger to do the dance numbers in the show. A friend of mine, who was becoming a model, taught me how to "eat without consequences." I went through several months of bulimia, until it began to cause damage to my vocal cords.

I was still desperate to stay thin, so as soon as I would gain three pounds I would starve five more off of myself. The seventies ideal was to be as skinny as Twiggy, the first-ever supermodel. I wasn't thinking about the health consequences. No one seemed to be. The shocking death of my friend in the entertainment business Karen Carpenter, in 1983, was the first time the public really became aware of eating disorders.

I didn't continue those eating habits after the variety show ended, but I never looked in a mirror without analyzing my weight and mentally criticizing myself for not being stick-thin. Still today, there are times when I view myself through harsh eyes. A lifelong habit is tough to break completely and I still have some long-term consequences from my radical approaches to losing the weight.

After the birth of my youngest son, Matthew, in 1999, I began to open my eyes to the extremely negative effect that my public "role model" image had on the self-esteem of women who paid attention to my life. I had my baby halfway through the eight-week break between season one and season two of the *Donny & Marie* talk show, leaving me less than four weeks to lose the sixty pounds (yes, 6-0!) I had gained in pregnancy and to fit back into my wardrobe again. I didn't make it. (Hmmm . . . perhaps a severe bout of postpartum depression held me up a bit. Talk about being put through the wringer! I felt as two-dimensional and emotionally flat as wet laundry.)

I had to shoot press photos for the billboards and magazine ads for the second season while I was still nine months pregnant. I had a lot of extra poundage from one set of cheeks down to the other. The solution was to dress me in black and then alter the photo by digitally removing my pregnancy and all the extra pounds from my face, my arms, my waist, and my backside. The results were pretty impressive. I looked better than I did before I got pregnant and I was grateful for modern technology. I wanted to try the same thing at home. It didn't work. My butt wouldn't fit into the scanner! It really ticked me off!

The day we returned to the studio my assistant gave me a stack of fan letters and e-mails that had arrived. Many were congratulations on the baby, but there was a large handful that really caught my attention. They each contained a different version of the same message: "I had my baby the same time you had yours. You look fabulous but I still have a lot of extra weight to lose. How did you do it? What's wrong with me? Why can't I drop these pounds?"

I felt as though I had sent scores of postnatal women to the back corners of their closets to cry in shame. I wanted to write to each of them personally. Nothing was wrong with them. It's completely natural to have extra weight after giving birth. The body needs time to recover. Knowing that the altered photos of me looking slender two weeks after giving birth were making new mothers feel bad broke my heart and changed my mind forever about body image.

My mother imparted this bit of wisdom to me a number of years ago. She said, "You spend the last half of your life fixing what the first half did to you."

Now I know she was absolutely right, but I'd like to believe that we could shake the earth with thinking differently about our weight and focusing more on how true beauty comes from being healthy, both physically and emotionally.

I've decided that I'll no longer flee the thought of having a true female body. And I'm going to stand and fight for my own daughters to be healthy, no matter what their natural body size. I wish I could have all the countless hours back that I spent worrying about my weight or believing the media-supported illusion of what constitutes a perfect woman. I'm not embarrassed by my weight anymore. I'm more concerned about wasting another moment of precious life on self-criticism.

Sure, I'll still carry on my makeup when I fly to make sure I have lip liner for touch-ups and powder to conceal the red veins on the sides of my nose, and I'll still hold in my stomach when I'm in front of a group of people, but I won't hold in my thoughts about how important it is to love and accept yourself as you are. Then, when the ground moves and you find yourself out on the lawn, you don't have to pack up your self-esteem. It will carry you forward through anything that comes your way.

And, as a side note: Your seventy-two-hour emergency survival kit should never contain an eighteen-hour girdle.

WXR-Pee

Each year for Halloween, I go green as Witchelina. The year I did my radio show, Donny dressed up as me. Scarier than my witch garb by far, mostly because he has better legs than mine!

Osmond Family Archive

Here's the major benefit of having a radio show: Wake up. No makeup. All you need to be ready for work is your voice and a sense of humor. Being heard but not *seen* sounded like heaven to me, especially after growing up in a business where it was unfathomable to have a blemish. One zit was enough to get me sent to a dermatologist when we were doing the original *Donny and Marie* show. The culprits were vacuumed out, sometimes weekly. To this day, my pores still cringe when I turn on the Hoover to clean the carpet!

In the fall of 2003, a national radio company approached me with an offer to host my own syndicated afternoon show. They suggested the show be broadcast right from my neighborhood in Utah. I immediately said "yes" and "thank you."

A studio was built into the top floor of the

building where my office was located, and along with a three-person staff and a handful of interns from the local universities, *Marie and Friends* hit the radio waves.

I've always had a love for radio. The public's awareness of my brothers' music skyrocketed in the 1970s because of radio. I'll never forget the day their career was truly launched. We were in our church's parking lot on a Sunday morning, listening to the popular DJ Casey Kasem count down to the number-one song on his show, *American Top 40*. Our father had let us duck out of the service a bit early knowing that "One Bad Apple" was somewhere on the charts. None of us had any idea what number it would be.

As Casey announced song number nine, number six, number four, we wondered if it might have already been played while we were in church. Casey announced the number-two song, "Knock Three Times" by Tony Orlando and Dawn. My brothers looked at each other, barely daring to have a what-if expression on their faces. When my father got excited about anything, he would make sniffing noises, and now his nose was going crazy. Then there was a 120-minute commercial break (really only ninety seconds or so, but it seemed much longer), and the anticipation to hear who took the top spot on the countdown was nearly unbearable.

I remember Casey finally coming back on the air to say, "The number-one song in America is the Osmond Brothers with 'One Bad Apple.'"

We all whooped and hollered and jumped around the car and a couple of my brothers actually screamed. After that week, their concert schedule doubled, their fan base quadrupled, and it was the teenage girls who were screaming, not my brothers. Well, to be honest, Jay has been known to shriek a time or two. I'd hate to embarrass him by describing an incident in the Genting Highlands resort when some moths flew out from the opened curtains. That's for Jay to tell — not me.

Radio helped to create the same "overnight" success for me two years later when I was thirteen years old and "Paper Roses" went to number one on the Country and Billboard charts. I got the news backstage at my brothers' sold-out Madison Square Garden concert. I started to cry, but I don't think it was from happiness. It was mostly from fear, as I remember it, because Alan said, "Find something to wear, Marie. You're going onstage to sing your hit song tonight." Little did Alan know that his request would make everything change so rapidly, not just my pulse rate. I had been onstage many times before, but never to sing completely alone. After my debut that night I began touring with my brothers full-time and the name of the group had to be changed from the Osmond Brothers to the Osmonds. Yes, one of the original boy bands had permanently been infiltrated by a little girl power.

I already knew how much radio could change the life of a recording artist, but it wasn't until I hosted my own show that I found out how much the listeners could change my perspective on life, too.

My show business friends came through for me with heartfelt and funny interviews. Wynonna called in from her tour bus and we talked about our common lives: growing up in the business, being moms, and dealing with weight issues. Larry King and I discussed baseball and fatherhood, his life-threatening circumstance with heart disease, and his own growing up without a dad. Mary Hart and I had fun singing in Swedish and chatting about her favorite Christmas memories, and even hard-to-get Garth Brooks came out of retirement for twenty minutes to catch up with me on the air about his decision to divorce, his love for his daughters, life with Trisha Yearwood, and his Halloween pranks. There were many other celebrity interviews, all interesting, but what I looked forward to most was talking to the daily listeners and hearing their unforgettable stories. Every day at the studio I laughed like crazy and shed some tears, too. You name the topic and chances were the phone lines would light up with true-life stories that were more compelling than any Hollywood studio could produce.

With almost one in four Americans living as single adults now, one of the big topics was dating and trying to find love.

One woman called in to complain that she would never go on a blind date again. A friend had set her up with a guy who seemed a little quiet and shy, but very nice. They went out for sushi and then to a movie. After the movie, she invited him to her condo for dessert. He offered to clear the coffee cups to the kitchen before he left. At the door he leaned toward her for a good-night kiss and a block of cheese fell to the floor and hit her shoe. She said she recognized the half pound of smoked cheddar because she had bought it earlier that day. Her blind date had stolen it from her fridge.

It's a good thing this caller was laughing, too, because I couldn't stop.

"Where did the cheese fall from?" I asked, in disbelief.

"I think it was tucked into his pants," she answered.

I couldn't stop myself from saying, "Gosh, I'd hate to imagine where he was hiding your crackers."

Then, another woman called in to say that her date the night before had literally pocketed the cheese right in front of her. They had been in a Mexican restaurant, and when her date noticed she hadn't finished her cheese quesadilla, she offered it to him. He wrapped the uneaten quesadilla in a napkin and put it into the breast pocket of his suit coat as she watched in total horror.

I told her, "Maybe he was planning to take you salsa dancing later!"

Soon another woman called in to say: "At least she got to go on the date." She was a single woman in her fifties who decided to go by herself to visit New York City and see some Broadway shows. While riding a stationary bike at a crowded YMCA, she spotted a nice "balding but cute" man who was lifting weights. He began to flirt with her a bit, much to her delight. As she said, "He was single and I had been through a bad breakup three months earlier. It was really fun to flirt again. Earlier that morning I had asked God to give me a sign if it was time to date again."

After exchanging the basic information of name, jobs, and home state, she decided to head to the locker room to get cleaned up. She washed up, reapplied her makeup, and took a couple more minutes to fix her hair.

She said on air: "I was going the extra mile because I was certain he was going to ask me out before I left the gym. I was really looking forward to a fun evening in Manhattan . . . with a man!!!"

As she entered the gym, she saw two paramedics hovering over a body on the floor, doing CPR. She looked around for her new friend to find out what had happened, then she realized that it was him they were working on. A woman exercising nearby said that he had keeled over unconscious as soon as she had left the room.

The caller said when the paramedics lifted him onto a gurney and rushed him out the door, she had to wonder if she "had missed the more subtle signs that maybe it wasn't time to date again."

Then she asked me if I had ever been on a bad blind date. I had to admit to one, although it wasn't a disaster because of the guy. I was the one who made him want to wipe me out of his memory bank forever, I'm certain.

About a year after "Paper Roses" became a hit, my brothers and I were out on a tour. Our popularity was really growing rapidly and we were playing sold-out venues across the country. During the summers we often played to huge state fair crowds. At one of these shows I was introduced to a really cute boy whose father was working backstage. My parents didn't allow any of us to date until we were sixteen, but that evening after our show, my mother said that I could go on some of the carnival rides with this boy, his friend, and a girlfriend of mine who was traveling with us at the time. I have a tendency to laugh more when I'm nervous. Usually it's a good way to release energy, but that night, something completely unexpected happened.

The four of us were in a funhouse attraction with crooked stairways, trick mirrors, and a steep, moving ramp that led to the top of an enclosed circular slide.

My girlfriend, who was trying to be so mature in her miniskirt, was having a hard time being graceful with all of the obstacles and unsure footing. As we stepped onto the ascending ramp, she turned to look at the boy who was her date. That's when she slipped and sat down hard as the ramp continued taking us rapidly to the top. Because her feet were higher than her seat, she couldn't manage to stand back up, and it was all she could do to not roll backward. None of us could help her, either, as letting go of the railings would have caused us to topple over on top of her.

I'm horrible when it comes to someone falling down. I want to be kind, but my first reaction, if they are not injured, is to laugh. And laugh hard. My mother was the same way. It's her fault that I come by it naturally.

I burst out laughing. My girlfriend started to giggle, then guffaw. We couldn't stop, even though our dates seemed to be getting embarrassed by our snorting and gasping for air.

Finally, we got to the top of the incline and it was our turn to go down the slide. The boys let us go first and then they followed close behind.

By this time we were hopelessly hysterical, and then even our bladders gave up trying to remain dignified. Our poor dates slid right through the puddles we were leaving behind. Now a normal person might start to feel bad about this, but we both laughed even harder at what was happening. By the time we reached the bottom of the slide I knew I could never look the cute boy in the face again. I grabbed my girlfriend's arm as soon as our feet touched the ground and shouted, "Let's get out of here."

We ran all the way back to the tour bus, still laughing, though I'm sure the boys we left behind with pee-soaked jeans weren't all that amused.

The other bonus to doing a radio show, or even writing a book, is that you can admit to embarrassing experiences that you would never tell in person. However, somewhere out there is probably a fortysomething good-looking guy who still tells his buddies, face-to-face, the story of when Marie Osmond *didn't* leave him "high and dry."

Oh, well. At least no one had to call the paramedics.

LIVE FROM OREM

Two people who deserved applause for a job well done: our mother and father.

Osmond Family Archive

Before Robert Redford made Park City a destination spot for hip people who love independent films, my father and brothers decided to relocate our hit television show from Hollywood, California, to Orem, Utah.

It was a family vote. That was how we made all major decisions. Majority rules. The majority had voted to move to LA from Utah in the 1960s when Alan, Wayne, Merrill, and Jay were offered a contract on *The Andy Williams Show.* Ten years later, following the first season of the *Donny and Marie* variety show on ABC, the vote was on the table whether to move the family back to Utah. I was in the minority. I wanted LA.

It's 652 miles from Los Angeles to Orem, but for me, at age sixteen, I might as well have been traveling back to the year 652 B.C. (bye-bye, civilization!), because that's how isolated and out of touch the whole geographical location seemed to me. I had become a full-fledged LA girl. I couldn't fathom how my brothers were willing to give up our access to Beverly Hills shops and cutting-edge fashion and four-star restaurants and polluted haze for snowcapped mountains, fresh air, no traffic, and privacy. "What are they thinking???" I wrote in my journal, noting that something must truly be wrong with the way the male mind functioned.

Just when Yves Saint Laurent's hot new "peasant look" was taking over the LA fashion world, I was apparently going back to Utah to live like a peasant. Or at least it seemed that way to me.

As ancient legends tell it, many who made the journey before me, missing their Neiman Marcus fix, would go to the local pond in Utah and cry buckets of tears. Thus was created the great Salt Lake. Believe it or not.

I was leaving the land of sprawling consumerism for a half-a-block downtown that had a fabric store, a drugstore, a hair salon, one shoe store, and a couple of apparel shops. Not one single pair of Jordache jeans (the trendiest denim of 1976) could be found for fifty-five miles! There was no Rodeo Drive in Utah, only rodeo clowns.

There were no cell phones yet, or instant

messaging or World Wide Web, in either LA or Orem, but at least in LA the lead story on the evening news wasn't about an agriculture class raising alpacas.

Driving wagon-train style in our packed-up cars towing multiple trailers along I-15, heading northeast across the desert, I knew that I was saying good-bye to the exciting lifestyle that I was really just getting into. Now, as a parent, I can see how that was the main reason my father wanted to get us "out" of LA. Donny and I were the youngest-ever television hosts (and we still hold that record), and between us we had an estimated value of over $40 million. But our estimated value didn't matter to our parents — our values did.

Our parents weren't concerned if we understood high fashion, gourmet food, how to pose for the paparazzi, or the newest "glam rock" music craze. They wanted us to be people of integrity with a rock-solid foundation in faith and family. They knew that the value of both is more easily understood through working hard and having a humble heart. Heaven knows I had worked hard to keep us residing in LA, but now my heart was definitely being humbled on that road to Utah.

The Osmond Studios were built and the

Donny and Marie show started a new season . . . taped live in Orem, Utah, with Mount Timpanogos replacing the famous Hollywood sign as the scenery we saw every day on our way to work. Mount Timpanogos resembles the profile of a sleeping woman. Other legends tell (and I'm not kidding on this one) that the mountain was named for an Indian maiden who died of grief after being forced to separate from her love. I wondered if she was forced to leave LA, too.

Our new studio became the venue for new life lessons. Not only did my brothers and I perform in the shows, but we performed almost every task needed to make the shows happen, from choreographing dance numbers to stocking concessions, engineering the sound, writing songs, and even painting the walls. Our new catered food meant remembering to boil a couple of eggs before we left home for the day and bringing them to the studio with us. Any time we didn't have a microphone in hand onstage, chances were we were holding a toilet brush or a broom and putting it to use backstage. In the course of an hour I could go from being in the spotlight wearing a Bob Mackie designer gown to sporting bright yellow gloves designed by Rubbermaid, scrubbing the spots off the bathroom mirrors.

One night I arrived back home, exhausted from a full day of studying my schoolwork with a tutor, then rehearsing songs, sketches, and dance moves. I was ready for one thing — collapsing in bed.

My mother greeted me at the door, her face full of enthusiasm and her hands powdered with white flour.

"Hi, honey. Are you ready to learn to bake bread? This will be a good skill to know when you have children. Singing to them won't fill their hungry tummies," she said, pointing me to an extra apron hanging from a hook near the stove.

"It's ten o'clock at night!" I protested.

She replied, unfazed, "Remember the earthquake? Ten o'clock. It's a good time to get busy." We were always taught to respect our mother, no matter what. But it didn't mean I couldn't "think" things.

Once I got past the thought "No one expects Olivia Newton-John to knead dough at the end of a long day," I actually began to enjoy the process. Bread making is elemental: the flour, the salt, the yeast, the honey, and the water, very back to basics. In her wisdom, my mother knew that if I could appreciate the ingredients, then I would never take the finished product for granted. She was wise enough to engage me in an activity where working with our hands gave us the opportunity to speak from the heart. And once in a while we could take out some frustrations with a punch or two to the rising dough. I loved those times my mom and I would talk together.

It's a beneficial approach I've used many times with my own teenagers. The best way to get them to "download" is to get them busy with a project. (I use crafting, cooking, sewing, playing board games, rearranging furniture, making smoothies in the blender, anything that does not involve a computer.)

Our bread, fresh from the oven, didn't last long once my brothers picked up the scent. No wonder, to this day, I can never go to sleep before one a.m. My ingrained behavior pattern is coaxing me: "It's ten o'clock!!! Let's make something. Cinnamon rolls!"

My father, with his military background, could be a tough taskmaster, as well. But he wasn't just being tough for the sake of it. He always wanted his children to be able to handle any situation with common sense and some elbow grease. My brothers and I commiserated and laughed together about having to do things like stock the paper towels, put away costumes, sweep the floors, and carry out the trash, but no matter what the chore we were all still working together, persevering, figuring out the best way to accomplish a goal that served the entire group. I understand now that he was really working our heart muscles.

A number of journalists, biographers, and entertainment professionals have commented on the Osmond endurance in show business, where fifteen minutes of fame is more often the rule of thumb. As I think about it now, we may have had a run of great "star" years if we had stayed in LA, but the move back to Utah and the chance to ponder the meaning of my life under those starry mountain skies changed me permanently. Those young, hard years gave us the backbone, determination and the kind of "work until it's all done" ethic that gave us a shot at lasting in the entertainment business for decades.

A year or two before my mother could no longer travel due to the effects of her strokes, she came for one of her many visits to be with her "grandbabies." My kids loved to have Grandma stay at our house because she always had a fun project or two . . . or three or four . . . ready to go. One evening, I arrived home from the airport after signing dolls at a retail store in North Carolina. It was past the kids' bedtime, so I expected to come in to a sleeping household, climb the stairs and crawl into bed. Much to my surprise, Jessica and Rachael, who were preteens at the time, met me at the door, their shirts splotched with flour. Brianna and Brandon, the toddlers, were close behind and grabbed me around the knees with jelly-covered hands.

"We made bwwwed!" Brandon grinned up at me. "Wiss Gwwwannma! And me. And Waychol. And Yessika. And Bweeauna. And Bweeauna's verwee messy."

And I said: "Wealwee?"

With eight children, you learn to speak each of their languages. Is there a Rosetta Stone for that?

The aroma in the air almost made me cry with joy. I couldn't wait to sit down with my mom and kids and have a warm slice with melting butter and jelly. That's when my mother walked toward me, drying off her hands with a dish towel, and said, "Take a nice, long whiff. Because that's all that is left!" The bread that took ninety minutes to make only lasted for three minutes before being devoured by my children. It was okay by me. I was pretty sure that even though they had scarfed down every bit of fresh baked bread, they had hopefully ingested some of the extremely valuable age-old life lessons that I had learned from my mom too.

My mother put a pan of milk on the stove to make me some hot chocolate as a consolation prize. And though she was yawning and tired from giving hours of time and attention to my young children, she still wanted to hear all about my day. As we dunked marshmallows under the warmed milk in our mugs, she said, "It's ten o'clock. We can talk while we clean out the storage room."

I miss you, Mom!!!

LET IN THE JOY

The perfect final appearance for my brothers' Fiftieth Anniversary in Entertainment tour and celebration. We had the great privilege of performing with the Mormon Tabernacle Choir. As pictured, from left to right, all of my dear brothers. Seated: Tom, Alan, Wayne, Virl. Standing: Merrill, Jimmy, Donny, Jay.
Courtesy of Mormon Tabernacle Choir, © IRI, 2009

"Who is that?!" my preschooler, Abby, asked me, crinkling her nose in confusion as she pointed to a man who looked absolutely lost in the middle of Chicago's Midway Airport. He was smoothing down his wispy white hair across the top of his head as his eyes intently took in the crowd. His face looked eager and endearing in a way that I recognized well.

"He's your uncle," I said, hoisting a *Dora the Explorer* wheelie bag onto the security scanner. "Remember?"

"Another one?" Abby asked me, astonished.

"Yes, sweetheart. Your uncle Wayne."

"Uncle Wayne," Abby repeated, very seriously. "Why does he keep going around in circles?"

I told her, "Oh, he's just looking for someone who will listen to his jokes."

"Don't smile at him, Abigail!" my older

teenager instructed her youngest sister. "I've already heard all of the jokes and I can't fake laugh right now." Rachael tugged her newsboy cap down almost over her eyes, which were suffering from a five a.m. wake-up call. Knowing that Wayne takes any eye contact as an invitation to spill out his endless library of one-liners, she attempted to discourage the barrage.

Abby tucked her face behind the hem of my coat and peeked out at Wayne with engrossed curiosity.

"Rachael, stop," I said. "You're going to make Abby think Wayne is crazy."

"Me?" Rachael responded. "Me? You always introduce him as 'My Crazy Brother, Wayne.' You did it on *Oprah,* Mother!"

She's right. I did. But it wasn't meant as an insult. After all, it takes one to know one.

Wayne walks, talks, and breathes jokes. He consumes jokes like my kids consume pizza-flavored Goldfish crackers, by the mouthful. Voice mails from Wayne are always three or four one-liners, followed by the real reason for calling. Wayne loves the sound of laughter as much as I do. I couldn't love him more.

"I'm entitled to tease him. I'm his sister," I said, defending my behavior.

Abby tugged on my purse strap. "Mommy,

Uncle Jimmy is your brother, too. Right?"

My little Abby was trying her best to figure out her family ties, and our trip to Chicago to appear on Oprah's show was like a two-day crash course in Osmond connections.

Oprah had us on her show to commemorate the Osmonds' fiftieth anniversary in entertainment. She chartered a large commercial jet to fly our family all together, had three huge buses to transport us, rented out an entire hotel to house us, brought in a "mile-long" buffet table and trucked in acres of food (!) to feed us: over one hundred Osmonds, plus about twenty extra people, including mothers-in-law, assistants, managers, and a babysitter or two.

As Oprah had reminded her audience: It all started in 1961 with Alan, Wayne, Merrill, and Jay performing in their first appearance at Disneyland. Since then, members of the Osmond family have collectively sold over 150 million records, had numerous number-one singles (individually and together), hosted scores of television episodes, founded national charities, produced touring shows, headlined Las Vegas shows, opened a theater in Branson, written books, and started multiple businesses.

The branches on our family tree have

never been pruned! It all seemed impossible to describe to Abby how her grandma and grandpa had nine children: eight boys and one girl, her uncles and her mommy. And those nine children went on to have fifty-five children, Abby being one of the youngest. And those fifty-five children have now had forty-nine children of their own, with one or two or seven new ones appearing every year.

As I said on *Dancing with the Stars* when asked if I thought I had a chance to win from the call-in votes: The show has 25 million viewers, and 22 million are Osmonds!

However, as I kicked off my flip-flops to walk through the airport metal detector (I wore sandals for months after *Dancing with the Stars,* trying to help the skin grow back on my feet), I wasn't thinking about the 25 million viewers who watch *Dancing with the Stars,* or the 7 million who watch Oprah each day. I found myself thinking about two people only — two people who are finally together again. My heart was so full of admiration for the two who were somehow responsible for every person boarding that private airplane to return to Salt Lake City. Whatever each Osmond has become individually has bloomed from the legacy these two built together. I was overwhelmed with missing them both: my mother and father, Olive and George Osmond.

It had been the most bittersweet week of my life. On Monday, I was so excited to perform a *Dancing with the Stars* tribute to my parents, to one of their favorite songs, "Boogie Woogie Bugle Boy." My dance partner, Jonathan Roberts, and I dressed in the military style that my dad wore when he first courted my mom by taking her to a Tommy Dorsey big-band dance. They were so good together that they would often win dance competitions, which supplemented their income in their first year of marriage.

He loved that I was doing a show featuring ballroom dancing. As I always did, I called him an hour before the show aired to make sure he was watching. He always was.

The next morning, Daddy got up, took a shower, got dressed, straightened up his room, lay back on his bed, and covered himself with an afghan I had knitted for him years before. He smiled and passed sweetly away at age ninety. He was supposed to be with us on Oprah's show, celebrating our fifty years in show business, but I think he knew his earthly work was done. As I told Oprah, "My dad wanted to go dance with my mother again. They are Dancing 'in' the Stars."

I ran my fingertips through Abby's silky baby hair. I thought about how the next day she would go to my daddy's funeral with me. As sad as Abby would be about saying good-bye to Grandpa, I knew that within a year or so her memories of time spent with him would fade. At her tender age, her growing mind expands by the minute with all the new discoveries and knowledge that will carry her into her future. One day, along with all of God's children, she will be the hope of the future of the world, too. That didn't seem possible as I watched her, flapping her arms and perching on one leg, like a flamingo with a Cherry Twizzler hanging from her mouth, crazy for a good laugh. My brother Wayne looked on with a grin of approval. And I thought, "Ah, yes . . . the Osmond legacy lives on."

My heart was rushed by an emotional whirlwind from accepting that I no longer had my parents, and from an awareness of a new place I would now fill in the family, the matriarch of the Osmond men.

When I felt I could finally explain the Osmond family to Abby, she had completely lost interest and was kneeling on the floor, whispering secrets that were obviously hysterically funny to her cousin Bella, my brother Jimmy's youngest child. As I watched the two little girls giggling together, I could feel the warm presence of my parents. It was like they were with my brothers and me the entire time, in the same way that they had told each of us that God is watching over all of His children. I could feel them lovingly watching over their children and grandchildren and great-grandchildren, all together. I would have loved to have been Daddy's little girl and my mother's only daughter again, if only for a moment, but I knew they were comforting me. I could almost hear them whispering in my ear: "This is the cycle of life, Marie. Let in the joy."

BORROWED BLING

The only photo of the necklace I'll never forget.
Osmond Family Archive

I'm a woman who feels something is missing if I'm not wearing jewelry. Before I leave the house I always check to make sure that my nose and forehead don't shine but that something on my neck and ears does. *Bling!* I never go to a pharmaceutical counter for a mood elevator; I go to a jewelry counter. A twenty-eight-dollar pair of earrings is bliss when you're having a bad day.

I'm pretty certain it was Elizabeth Taylor who launched the bling competition between celebrities. It was her red-carpet walk at the 1970 Oscars, when she wore a 69-carat Cartier diamond pendant that had the world asking, "What violet eyes?" Nothing within five city blocks could take the attention away from Liz Taylor's ice. I was about ten years old that year and pretty impressionable, too. I have to wonder if Liz's megadiamond planted the seed of my own fascination with all things that sparkle.

Today, every Hollywood red carpet is like a showcase for famous jewelry designers, who invite the stars who are attending to "borrow" some gems. And many of us, with the possible exception of Oprah, who probably never even borrows library books, usually do. It's pretty fun to wear forty thousand dollars of Harry Winston, Chanel, or Tiffany diamonds on each earlobe and a cool quarter million in precious gems around your neck. Of course, the possibility of a piece of borrowed jewelry falling off and your not realizing it is incredibly nerve-racking. Unless it's heavy enough for you to tell it's on without looking, you can end up touching your ears and neckline more than a third-base coach at the World Series. Besides that, the jeweler bodyguards follow you everywhere. I saw a pair of black men's shoes outside of my stall in the ladies' room at the Emmy Awards. Hey!

Just like the World Series, it's a relief to have it locked up until the next season.

A Saudi princess once gave me the most valuable piece of jewelry I had ever owned. It wasn't really a gift, per se, it was more like a "get."

Donny and I were headlining along with our brothers at the Hilton in Las Vegas. Every show was a sellout due to the popularity of our TV variety show. Being a young girl, I had no idea who the numerous so-called important people were that we were introduced to each evening, everyone from Vegas high rollers to film stars to foreign dignitaries. The reason it didn't faze us was that our parents taught us that every person we meet is equal in importance in God's eyes. It didn't matter if the person had just stepped out of a Rolls-Royce in the City of Light or a pickup truck at the Iowa State Fair.

As a teenager, I understood that every person was equal, but I could see that every piece of jewelry was not! I spotted her gorgeous necklace the moment I met the Saudi princess, who was a big fan of our variety show.

Positioned perfectly in the clavicle indentation in her neck was a stunning four-leaf-clover pendant. It was 18-carat gold with a 1-carat diamond directly in the center of four leaves paved with diamond chips. I couldn't take my eyes off of it.

"Your necklace is absolutely breathtaking," I told her. "I love it!"

What really left me gasping for air was when she replied, "Then you must have it."

With great casualness, as if passing along a string of plastic Mardi Gras beads, she reached up and unhooked her necklace and dropped it into my hand.

I'm pretty sure my mouth was insisting that I couldn't accept it, though I doubt I was very convincing. I have no memory of chasing her down to give it back after she smiled and walked away.

My first thought was, "This is really mine!" followed by what seemed incomprehensible to me: "Imagine having so much money that you can give away diamond necklaces."

That four-leaf-clover necklace became my prized possession. I never had it appraised, but I'm certain it was worth thousands. More important than that, it made me feel like a million dollars. I wore it everywhere and with everything, except my show costumes. Every night, before I went onstage, I would take it off and put it in a little drawer in the dressing room. It was the last thing I took off and the first thing I put back on after the show.

One night, while I was onstage, someone decided to clean out the dressing room. Literally. When I pulled open the little drawer, the necklace was gone. The possession that I thought I would never part with had parted with me!

I tried to apply the advice my mother had

always given us about items that had gone missing. She would always say: "I guess they needed it more than we do." Her wisdom wasn't working this time. I couldn't have been angrier. Visions of my necklace being pawned by someone who didn't care about what it meant to me stormed through my mind. Four-leaf clovers are for luck. This one was obviously bad luck.

I was furious for days, observing every person backstage with total suspicion. Who was it? With about forty people involved in every show, on top of all the people who worked at the hotel, it would be impossible to ever know. Over and over I thought, "How dare someone take my diamond necklace? It was mine."

Then, unexpectedly, a thought tugged at my conscience: "You first took the necklace from her." Even though I didn't steal the necklace, I realized that I did take the necklace from the princess, never knowing if it held any special meaning for her. I never even asked. I wanted it, so I rationalized that she must be so wealthy that she could let go of her necklace and never miss it. Whoever took the necklace from me may have thought the same way. "Oh, she's a celebrity. She can get whatever she wants."

Although this thought didn't take away

the pain of losing the necklace, it did lessen the anger and blame that had been left in its place. I was never going to get the necklace back, but I could tell that the bad feelings would stick to me forever unless I really let them go.

I had to let them go.

I've been given and even bought my share of fine jewelry since losing that four-leaf clover. I appreciate it, but I stay away from becoming attached. Diamonds are the hardest natural substance found on the earth and they represent eternal love, but in the realm of eternity, they're really just stones.

I will admit, when the occasion arises I still love to parade some loaner platinum on the red carpet, but that's for the movies and award shows, not for real life. I can't spend forty thousand dollars on a pair of earrings. Come on! That's a week's worth of groceries in my family!

SCATTERBRAIN

As a spokeswoman for Go Red for Women, my focus is on bringing awareness to heart health. I was ready for this appearance thanks to a red Sharpie.

The American Heart Association and Go Red For Women

"We're both scatterbrains."

That was the answer my oldest son, Stephen, gave when asked in what way he was most like me.

I happened to be standing nearby, autographing an album cover for a fan, and overheard his answer.

"I'm not a scatterbrain!" I protested, as I wrote a huge "Love, Marie Osmond" on the cover and returned it.

"You signed right on Donny's face," the fan said, in blunt disbelief, and then recovered quickly. "But that's okay. Thank you very much."

I apologized and then, before he walked away, I suggested that he should have Donny sign his autograph over my face so it could be a really bizarre collector item. I thought that was pretty quick thinking on my part.

Stephen grinned at me, like I had just

proven his "scatterbrain" indictment.

"Stephen, I was distracted momentarily by you and your insult. That's why I signed in the wrong place," I said, pointing the really expensive pen I was holding for emphasis.

"This is really pretty," I added, twirling the pen to see all angles of the etched silver plating. "Is it mine?"

"No. You forgot to give that guy his pen back." Stephen laughed, putting his arm around my shoulder. "By the way, Mom, did you see where I left my jacket?"

Great faith, kindness, and a sense of musicality are on the short list of attributes that I'd love to say Stephen could have inherited from me. Having spacey neurotransmitters is not one of them. In fact, I've never been called a scatterbrain before. Well, if I have, I don't remember it. I guess one person's scatterbrained is another person's busy. That's what I am. Busy. Busy in the extreme!

Find me a busy woman who hasn't had to call AAA more than twice in the same day because she keeps locking her keys in her car. I'm not alone in that, am I? In fact, as proof of the saying that the apple doesn't fall far from the tree, an AAA card was the most useful gift I ever gave my three older kids. Every time they use it, they think of me. So I know that's at least three times a week.

One day, as Big Dave, the AAA tow-truck driver, finished jimmying my door lock open, he said to me, "I'm going to go get a sandwich and wait for your next call. Can I bring you a roasted turkey on pumpernickel?"

I told him: "Oh, you're funny. No, thanks. I'm on my way home. You probably won't hear from me again until tomorrow."

I mean, if I truly fit the label of "scatterbrain," I would leave things behind after going through airport security, right? I've never once been called over the speaker system to come back for my computer bag, my wallet, or my neck pillow. I always have time to gather up my stuff while one of the very nice scanner people retrieves my shoes from the other side of the metal detector, where I left them on the floor near the stack of plastic bins.

When I was doing *Dancing with the Stars* I bought each of my kids a cell phone. I told them it was so they could always reach me, even on the set, and also so they would call in every single show to vote for Mommy. Having seven cell phones is very handy around the house, too. I can always ask one of the kids to ring my cell number so I can figure out where I left my phone. Do scatterbrains have *that* kind of common sense? Though I will admit, if every hotel in which I've left behind my phone charger cord for the past ten years all sent them back to me at once, it would fill a UPS truck.

Scatterbrain? I'm a creative thinker. I've had to be. As a spokesperson for the "Go Red for Women" campaign for the American Heart Association, I go on a publicity tour to raise awareness a couple of times a year. I always remember to wear red and pack a variety of red suits, shoes, and slacks. At the last event, we were in New York and running late for a live appearance on the *Today* show. Once we were in the car, I realized that I had left the earrings that match my red necklace back in the hotel room. It was too late to turn around. I scrambled in my bag and came up with one pair of light blue crystal earrings, which really didn't go with anything I had on.

I noticed that one of the talent coordinators riding with me was writing notes with a red Sharpie.

"Can I borrow your pen for a minute?" I asked her. In a flash, I had colored the crystals on the earrings with the red Sharpie, as the talent coordinator gasped, "That looks great, but didn't you just ruin your earrings?"

"A little witch hazel and they'll be as good as *blue*," I said.

"I take it you've done this before," she said and laughed.

"A variety of permanent markers should be a part of every woman's emergency kit," I advised her. "You can color in a scuff on black shoes, water down the red one a bit to use as a lip stain if you forgot your lipstick, darken a beauty mark with a dark purple or brown, or change the color of almost any kind of jewelry on the spot."

I choose to see this not as a scatterbrain moment of forgetting my earrings but as a fantastic opportunity to pass along really helpful emergency tips to another woman.

If Stephen has borderline forgetfulness that he believes he inherited from me, it's probably because I have my mother's DNA. She was a very busy woman, too, with the nine of us kids, our lessons and our laundry, her newsletters to the fans, bookkeeping, managing real estate sales, gardening, helping out at church, and countless other activities in which she was involved. Once in a while something would fall through the cracks . . . or seep out of the trunk of the car.

One hot summer in the early 1970s we came home to our ranch in Huntsville, Utah, after finishing an extensive tour. We looked forward to having time to be away from the crowds and back to nature, and would often stay put for a whole month, if time allowed.

About a week into our time off, Wayne announced, "The car in the driveway has a really bad odor coming from it."

Jay added, "I think something is leaking from it, too."

My father got up from the kitchen table and started to follow my brothers to check out the situation.

I was helping my mother clear dinner dishes when suddenly her eyes flew open wide.

"The groceries!" she said. "Oh, no!"

We dashed out into the driveway, just as Father was opening the trunk. There sat six bags of groceries that had accidentally been left to bake in a 100-plus degree trunk for a couple of days.

"I forgot, I shopped for food on my way home from the post office," my mother said, and then clapped her hand over her mouth, looking at the results.

Four gallons of ice cream had turned into a moldy lake in the bottom of the trunk.

The bag of potatoes had sprouted into small trees and some raw chicken legs and thighs were ready to get up and climb out on their own.

As much as my brothers tried to sanitize the trunk, it always carried the faint odor of rotting food, and no matter where the car was parked, flies seemed to hold their family reunions nearby.

Perhaps that's why station wagons are better for busy women. It's harder to forget that you grocery shopped because there is no trunk. Looking back, I know my mother must have really been overwhelmed because it was totally unlike her to ever forget that she bought ice cream. We are exactly alike in that way.

I really am not a scatterbrain. I only need to focus a bit more on the task at hand.

One evening, my fifth-grader, Brandon, was searching the room where I kept all of our crafting materials, desperate for a piece of poster board for a school project. He had forgotten it was due the next morning. As a mom who deals with minor emergencies all day long, I told him I'd make a quick run to the nearby discount store and be back in a flash.

When I arrived back home, Brandon met me in the driveway.

"That was a really long flash. You've been gone for two hours."

"I know," I told him. "Big Dave is on vacation, so they sent a different AAA guy. He took a while to get there. Help me carry in the bags."

"Bags?" Brandon asked.

"They were having some great sales."

Brandon carried the bags into the house and started to shuffle through my good deals: a twelve-pack of white crew socks, two-for-one ink cartridges for the printer, three cans of mixed nuts, a forty-eight-count box of granola bars, SPF 30 sunblock lotion, and a large plastic tub perfect for storing Christmas decorations.

After a minute he distracted me from trying to find my ringing cell phone in the bottom of my purse.

"Mom. Where's the poster board?"

Whoops.

Being a "creative" mom, I spent some time with Brandon recycling brown paper bags into substitute poster board. It was the best way to teach a lifelong, very useful lesson on resourcefulness and, more than that, he and I figured it out together.

A POSEIDON
ADVENTURE ON THE
LOVE BOAT

Calling Captain Stubing to the lido deck!
Osmond Family Archive

There was a lot of beauty and bluster the week I taped *The Love Boat* in Italy. One extremely strong gust nearly blew me overboard, but I managed to hang on. It wasn't the weather or even the ocean breeze that almost knocked me off my feet: it was a legendary actress.

Yes, I really did an episode of *The Love Boat*. It's pretty hard to comprehend that I would turn down the role of Sandy opposite John Travolta in the movie *Grease*, and then later agree to play a sheltered Italian girl on *The Love Boat*, but it's true.

Even now, thirty years later, some people I meet will still bring up my decision, and the fact that Olivia Newton-John achieved such major fame in the role that I turned down. They usually ask me about it with a quizzical look of disbelief, like: "What happened? I thought you didn't do drugs? Did you have a mental lapse?"

I'm sure it would have been a lot of fun to work with John Travolta and the talented cast, but I still have no regrets.

Even though the music was fun and the script was good, the ending of the story seemed to send a strongly mixed message to young girls, one that made me feel uncomfortable: the sweet "good girl" chooses to become a very different person due to peer pressure. As Rizzo sings in the movie, Sandy was "lousy with virginity." With the "cool" girls rating her moral values as a personal flaw, Sandy vows to change.

At the end of the movie, she appears as her transformed self in tight black pants, a revealing shirt, sassy high heels, a cigarette in hand, and an attitude of "come and get it."

This is the "happy" ending for Sandy — becoming exactly what her peers and boyfriend want her to be. From my perspective, it was not a story of a girl becoming a woman; it was a story of a girl becoming a sex object.

When the part was offered to me, I was still a teenager. Being in the public eye, I was watched closely by many other young people. Beyond that, however, I had been raised to believe that being a female was a blessing full of unique privilege. I see women as being the cocreators and nurturers of the future, the nucleus of the family. My parents had taught me that having self-respect as a woman could never be replaced by any amount of money, possessions, or popularity. It's something I want each of my own daughters to know, and something I learned a lot about in 1982 on the set of *The Love Boat.*

When I was offered the guest-star role of Maria Rosselli, one of the deciding factors for me was the chance to work with two incredible stage and screen legends: the funny and dear Ernest Borgnine, and the outrageously talented Shelley Winters. In the story line, the two of them were playing my cantankerous grandparents, who were journeying with me to meet my husband-to-be.

As timing would have it, my life was a bit similar to the character I was playing. I had recently become engaged to my first husband and I was very happy. I was twenty-two years old, looking forward to being a wife and a mother. I had so much enthusiasm about my future that I was like a sugar addict who gets the first piece of birthday cake with the giant rose made of frosting. I was buzzing with excitement.

My best friend, Patty, was along with me

as my traveling companion. When I wasn't on the set, Patty and I would go out and explore each city where the boat docked. We called it sightseeing. It was more like sighting the best stores and seeing how many we could get to before we had to be back to the ship. Let's just say the two of us have always done more than our share when it comes to stimulating the retail economy wherever we visit! She's the only one I know who can power shop at my pace.

About halfway through the week of filming, we were in Rome, Italy. I found the most beautiful christening gown I had ever seen in a small specialty shop. The handmade lace and the embroidered satin were breathtaking. I had to buy the gown to hopefully bless my own baby in someday.

I took it back to the set with me and was showing it to some of the friends I had made doing the show when Shelley Winters came over to see what everyone was *ooh*ing and *aah*ing over.

Shelley had been on edge with almost everyone equally, both cast and crew, the entire week. Now, for some reason, she flew into a rage over my purchase. I didn't understand and the crew stood stunned into silence as she ranted on about my "sentimental stupidity," scoffing at the baby gown.

I didn't even know how to respond. In total embarrassment, I gathered up my shopping bags and went to my room.

That night, the cast and crew traveled on to Venice. I spent the entire trip trying to figure out what on earth I had done that made Shelley Winters so furious. I thought that she had no reason to be so crabby. She had a great career and had won every award available in show business: an Oscar, a Tony, and an Emmy. In her younger years she was a Hollywood beauty. Now she was a first choice for a lot of high-profile, challenging character roles. It seemed to me that fortune had been generous to Shelley.

I decided it would be best to just ignore the incident and do whatever it took to get through the filming schedule. She obviously didn't like me at all.

The next evening, following a day of filming, there was a knock on my door. I wasn't expecting anyone, so I was even more surprised when I opened it to see Shelley standing there, cocktail in hand. It seemed, by the way she leaned on the door frame, that it wasn't her first one of the evening. After I invited her in she asked: "Can I see that baby gown you were showing everyone?"

I was actually afraid she would try to

destroy it, but I handed it to her anyway. She sat down in a chair with the dress in her hands, looking it over closely, not saying a word for the longest time. When she finally looked up, her eyes were full of tears. I didn't dare speak, until she said, "I have a daughter, you know."

I told her that I didn't know that.

Then Shelley scoffed, took a long gulp of her drink, and said, "I have so many awards I don't know what to do with them. I use them for doorstops. I could have had any man in Hollywood that I wanted."

She set her glass down hard on the table. I was concerned that she was building up steam again so I kept silent, not wanting to make her more upset.

"When my daughter was growing up, all I cared about was my career," she continued. "What would be my next big part? What role would get me further ahead? I guess my daughter felt like she was lost in the shuffle of my career."

Shelley's face softened for a moment and her chin quivered. "She hates me, you know."

Then she wiped her eyes and picked up her drink again.

"Here's to your career," she toasted me with a forced smile. "If you plan to have kids, which I hope you don't, but . . . if you do, I hope you'll remember what I'm telling you right now."

She stood to leave, hugged me, and then broke down sobbing in my arms.

"I would give back every single award I've ever won if I could have my daughter's arms around me right now."

She didn't even wait for me to respond. She picked up her glass and walked out the door, not turning to look back or say good night.

My heart broke for her.

When I anticipated working with Shelley, I thought I was going to have the opportunity to learn a lot about acting from a truly talented legend. What she gave me, though, was insight into what it means to be a woman and a mother, and a look into the painful emptiness of a broken relationship between mother and child. It was an extraordinary lesson at a very impressionable time in my life and my desired career.

I know I would have done a good job playing Sandy. I would probably have had a different career, with more film work or perhaps more hit records. I also know, however, that I would regret having my eleven-year-old daughter watch Mommy in that movie now, especially as she enters that time in her life when she is deciding what it means to be a female, and how to navigate in today's world all the expectations that may come her way when it comes to dating.

Every choice we make has an element of consequence. I guess the question in choosing is: Can you live with the results?

Maybe my guest-star turn on *The Love Boat* wasn't a career move that I happily highlight on my résumé, but it did help me dock in the reality that when the peer pressure, the awards, the applause, and even that fairy-tale marriage you think could never fail fades away, it's only self-respect that will keep you afloat through the storms.

NUN GAGS

"How do you solve a problem like . . . crooked lip liner and a French manicure on a young nun??"

Osmond Family Archive

I really sucked. At least my voice did. It sounded like I had sucked the air out of a helium balloon and then started to talk. Whenever I hear old television interviews or watch the early years on QVC from those snippets of videotape that they replay on every anniversary of *Marie Osmond Dolls,* I can't believe that sound is coming from me. It was tinny and high, like a cross between Gumby and a two-year-old.

I might have had that squeaker of a speaker for my entire life if my manager, Karl, who has been with me since my "Paper Roses" days, hadn't raised the rally flag for me to try performing Broadway shows in the early 1990s. At first, I resisted completely.

I was living in Nashville and touring by bus to do concerts across the country. I had quite the full operation to support: a country music band, a stage crew, lighting and sound crew, bus drivers, and a wardrobe person. We played the big venues and the honky-tonks, the state fairs and fall festivals.

My four children traveled everywhere with me as my second husband, Brian, didn't really care for country music or the South, and spent most of his time in Utah. He never wanted to be pegged as "Mr. Osmond," and I understood that. However, having to provide the family income, I didn't really have the option of being a stay-at-home Mrs. Blosil, either. I had worked hard to become a new Marie Osmond after the original *Donny and Marie* show. I was happy to finally be becoming an established country music artist. I was blessed by having recorded many country hits, like "Read My Lips," "No Stoppin' Your Heart," and the Grammy-winning "Meet Me in Montana," a duet with Dan Seals. And looking back now, it seems that was when I really began enjoying a solo career. I loved being with my children in my homelike bus, traveling from state to state to entertain country music fans. It was a pretty good life, as long as you didn't mind scraping a cow pie off your shoes once in a while, or repairing the amplifier wires when they were severed by horse hooves, or performing in an arena that thirty minutes earlier had been an auction block for about a hundred huge bulls. I've definitely heard some before, but never had to share a stage with bulls. *Elephants,* yes. When we started out as performers we were an opening Vegas act along with Tina and Bertha, mother and daughter gray elephants. I actually liked being around them. It was one place I felt petite!!

One evening, following a concert, Karl introduced me to Bob Young, an established and respected Broadway producer. Bob had flown in especially to encourage me to consider touring with a Broadway show. Though I was flattered, I couldn't imagine how my experience as an entertainer would work in any role except maybe *Annie Get Your Gun,* and I wasn't eager to set myself up to be compared to Ethel Merman or Mary Martin. No, thanks. It was tough enough trying to hold my own in a country market with brilliant artists I admired like Dolly Parton and Loretta Lynn.

It was Rachael, my youngest daughter at the time, who changed my mind. As we were getting ready to leave Nashville for another leg of the tour, she became violently ill. She was screaming in agony, but was too young to communicate what was wrong. My road manager put me and the other kids in the car and sped us to the Children's

Hospital emergency room. After hours of testing, it was discovered that Rachael had a kidney problem that could have eventually been fatal without treatment. I was exhausted, but relieved that it could be treated.

I called Karl from the hallway outside the ICU nursery. I asked him to please call the promoter of the next concert and explain that I had an emergency with my little girl and had to cancel. Five minutes later, Karl called me back, and with emotion choking his voice, he said, "Marie, they said they would sue you if you don't make the concert."

I was astounded that anyone would deliver an ultimatum to a mother with a child in a life-threatening situation. Only after the doctor assured me that they could stabilize my baby's condition could I even process what needed to be done. Knowing that I was my family's breadwinner and that I couldn't afford to be sued, I left a trusted babysitter at the hospital and boarded the tour bus with my other children. We had to drive three hundred miles through the night to make it to the concert venue. It was the longest, most painful night of my life as a mother. I arrived both distraught and tired, but I fulfilled my obligation to perform. We then immediately drove through the night again, to get back to my baby girl in Nashville.

I knew that I never wanted to have to choose between a child who needed me and a concert performance ever again. It was all the motivation I needed to make a life and a career change.

Karl arranged a meeting with the elated and darling Bob Young. From the moment we began talking, I knew Bob was a man who respected that many performers have families who matter greatly to them. He made a guarantee to me that my family could always come first in the case of any emergency, and that an understudy would be ready to take over at a moment's notice. He thought the perfect role for me to launch a Broadway career was as Maria in a new touring production of *The Sound of Music*. There would be children in the cast that my own children could play with, and a tutor on board for their educational needs. He even set the schedule to give me more than a month to rehearse before our first show went out on the road. I'm sure my hand was shaking as I signed the contract, but my heart knew it was the right choice.

Shortly after, I walked into my first rehearsal at a rehearsal studio right off of

Broadway in New York. I not only felt out of my league, I knew I wasn't even in the same sport anymore. My director was Jamie Hammerstein, the son of Oscar Hammerstein II, the man who wrote the lyrics to *The Sound of Music* and many other famous musicals. Talk about an intimidating debut in a Broadway show!! After meeting Jamie and the rest of the cast, I motioned for Karl to step into the hallway with me.

"Karl, this might be a mistake," I said. "These are professional Broadway actors."

Just as he's always done, he calmed me down through his utter belief in me.

"I know you can do this," he said. "You can't be afraid of what you don't know. What do you have to lose?"

It doesn't matter how many successes a performer may have had in the past, there's still some fear in trying an unfamiliar form of entertainment. Standing in that hall with Karl I could feel my confidence shutting down, but I knew if I backed out of the commitment, I'd regret it forever.

As the rehearsal pianist warmed me up, it was obvious that I was unprepared to switch gears from my country voice. I was pretty certain that Rodgers and Hammerstein never imagined the Austrian postulant, Maria, with a down-home twang as she scooped the notes through her songs. ("The Heeels Ahwre Ahhlllaaaheeeve!") I sounded more like a nun from the Smoky Mountains than the Austrian Alps. Did they have banjos in Salzburg convents in 1938?

At first, the cast members were somewhat reserved with me. They had to be wondering if I was just another celebrity trying her hand at a Broadway show. It only took a day or two to let them know that I was open to any and all suggestions for making my little nun . . . fly!

Once they realized that my goal was to really become a legitimate stage performer, they showered me with kindness. Some of the kindest words were suggestions of how to get help (not mental help . . . although taking on a Broadway leading role, I could have used some), which came from the ladies playing my fellow nuns. They directed me to Barbara Smith Davis, a cast member who was also an inspired vocal coach. Working extensively with her for hours before and after each rehearsal, I learned to retrain my voice for the stage. She taught me the proper technique for supporting big Broadway songs night after night without a microphone. How funny, I thought, that I would never have been able to record country or even pop music if I had first been professionally trained. You can take a raw voice and train it with technique, but it's nearly impossible to take a technically trained voice and revert it to that raw quality necessary for modern music. (It's a testament to Barbara's talent and range as a coach that she's recently helped me make another transition, from Broadway to my most current passion, singing opera. What can I say? Osmonds love a good challenge.)

In addition to the voice work, there was the process of figuring out my personal Maria look. The producers thought it might be a good idea for me to wear a blond wig.

Their argument was that people expected the character of Maria to look like Julie Andrews in the movie version. My eyes are deep chocolate brown and my skin tone goes with my eyes, so wearing a blond wig I looked about as natural as Smurfette.

I did try the wig out for our preview performances, but during the intermission, the theatergoers in the lobby were asking, "Who's the blond understudy for Marie Osmond?"

With my newly trained voice, I not only didn't sound like me, I didn't look like me, either. After one week the blond wig was eighty-sixed . . . and so was my Captain von Trapp. My first "Captain" was an actor from a popular science fiction movie. He was a sweetheart of a guy, a good actor, but not a singer. He couldn't hold the key. As the music is written, he was to always sing the melody and Maria was to harmonize with him. As soon as I began to sing the harmony, he would lose the melody and sing harmony with me. I would then quickly switch music parts so the audience would hear the correct melodics of the song when, seconds later, he would change parts again to join me in singing the melody. I couldn't follow his lead, because he couldn't sing the lead. By the time we previewed in Boston, his ship had docked for good. I'm pretty sure he was relieved.

My long-running Captain, Neal Benari, was a true Broadway pro. He has played many major musical roles, from Sweeney Todd in *Sweeney Todd* to Tevye in *Fiddler on the Roof.* He was unassuming, humble, had a great sense of humor, and was so much fun to perform with, especially if things went wrong on stage. In live theater, it's more realistic to say *when* things go wrong because it can be counted on to happen. Neal and I had the same "the show must go on" attitude. He barely missed a performance, and in the two years we toured I only had to use an understudy twice. We went on every night, even if we felt like the edge of death. Of course, there were some nights we both wanted to die . . . of embarrassment.

Following the scene in which Captain von Trapp asks Maria to join him at the party that evening, we would leave the stage and dash to "quick change" booths just out of view of the audience. I only had sixty seconds to go from wearing Maria's "work" dress to evening attire. Neal had to be even quicker, making his entrance before me wearing a full tux with tails, greeting the party guests. One night I was scurrying to finish dressing, when a stage manager, in a panic, threw open my curtain.

"Hey!" I said, lifting my robe up in front of me quickly. "Did you ever hear of knocking?"

He looked perplexed and sweaty.

"Right. Sorry," he said, turning his face away, and then back again, and then away once more.

I started to laugh. "It's okay! It's kind of tough to knock on a curtain."

"Marie! Please. You've got to save Neal!" he said. His face was flushed with worry or embarrassment. I didn't know which one.

"What's wrong?" I asked, coming out of the booth, pulling on my dress. Neal was so stage savvy, it would take a lot to make him lose his concentration. The only thing I could think of was that someone had accidentally poked him in the eye doing the costume change. But as I peeked around the edge of the side curtain I could see that it wasn't a poke in the eye. It was a shirttail peeking out of his fly!

Poor Neal. In his hurry to quick-change into his tux he had not checked his zipper. His shirttail was sticking straight out like a flag of surrender.

The audience was gracious enough not to laugh out loud, but there was audible snickering as more and more people noticed what Neal hadn't.

It was time for my entrance and the stage manager grabbed my hand.

"Fix this!" he implored. "He's oblivious!"

The problem was that there was no way I could possibly signal to him until I was close enough. That wasn't until we danced together.

Jamie Hammerstein was very particular about being authentic to the time period in which the play was set. The costumes and the hairstyles reflected the era, and the choreography mirrored the dancing of that day.

The Laendler is a beloved Austrian folk

dance. One very specific aspect of it, which we made certain to maintain, is that once two dance partners lock hands, they never let go until the dance is finished.

I wanted to say something to Neal but he grabbed both my hands for our dance much sooner than he usually did and the music started up. We spun several times before I could get out the words "Your fly's down."

Of course, he couldn't drop my hands, especially to adjust his pants, so we danced on. The lighting crew adjusted by narrowing the spotlight, hoping to take the attention off the shirttail and focus it only on our faces, but it didn't really help the situation. Maria's face is supposed to be flushed with shy attraction during this dance, but it was actually Captain von Trapp who was bright red from flirting with humiliation!

It wasn't until the von Trapp children took the stage to sing "So Long, Farewell" that Neal was actually able to bring closure to the situation.

However, it did give a whole different twist to some of the lyrics of that song: "An absurd little bird is popping out to say cuckoo."

After the show Neal and I had a good laugh as I fell in love with the unpredictability of live theater.

Oh, well. Jamie Hammerstein told me early on in rehearsal that his father had never intended for Maria to come off as seriously as Julie Andrews had played her in the movie. After all, the lyrics the other nuns sing about Maria describe her as a "flibbertigibbet, a will-o'-the wisp, a clown."

I decided that my Maria should be a little unexpected. I felt that her passion for life is what got her into trouble. The actress who played Mother Superior and I choreographed many fun moments where Maria fell to her knees to repent. Of course, I'm not laughing so much about it now that I have a permanent floating chip in one knee from five pratfalls a night for two years!! When I met one of the real von Trapp daughters, she told me that her stepmother did everything in a big way. She was actually very tomboyish, athletic, and had a lot of spirit. I bet *she* was smart enough to wear kneepads.

To open the show, I decided to lie flat on the floor of the stage with my feet propped up against a tree. It took the audience a moment to find where the "singing voice" was coming from, but it was unexpected and fun. The crowds seemed to love having Maria suddenly appear from nowhere.

On the opening night of the actual run, I

271

took my place on the floor right before the curtain went up. It was the same stage on which Mary Martin had debuted as Maria in the original 1959 production. My heart was pounding in anticipation. I started to sing the intro to the song and then I drew in a deep breath to really belt out the refrain. Somehow an incredibly large piece of dust, or perhaps an old fake snowflake from a past Christmas show, drifted down from the lighting grid and was sucked right into my esophagus. I tried to swallow and only miss a few notes, but it stuck like a postage stamp right on my gag reflex. I started to cough uncontrollably. I quickly sat up, hoping I could clear my throat out, but nothing worked. The orchestra replayed the refrain again and then again.

By now, I was really coughing uncontrollably and my eyes were watering so much that tears streamed down my face. As I stood up, a couple of cast members extended their hands to help me offstage. The audience sat in stunned silence. The orchestra halted.

My understudy was there in a flash, pulling her apron on as she ran out to take my place onstage. I couldn't believe it was happening. The hills might be alive, but I was about to choke to death.

I ran into the offstage bathroom and, not being able to breathe, I threw up. Then, as quickly as it had all come on, it was over. I was fine. I wiped my eyes, straightened my habit, and signaled to the stage manager.

"I'm fine. Please. Let's restart the show. There can't be an understudy for opening night."

He agreed and the curtain came back down.

The poor understudy Maria never even got to sing a note, but I don't think she minded. She was pretty overwhelmed at the thought of doing the show to a sold-out crowd who had paid to see Marie Osmond as Maria.

Throughout that performance every cast member gave me an extra dose of support, their smiles and enthusiasm encouraging me to forget about the opening debacle. The energy onstage was phenomenal and the audience caught the fever and rose to their feet at the curtain call.

I was thankful the next day that the newspaper notices were really positive, and not even one theater reviewer made a pun like "Marie Osmond Chokes as Nun."

It's often the mishaps in life that are remembered most fondly when you look back. Good times can be experienced and enjoyed by all, but it's those bumps in the road that really bond people together as family.

In the well-known story line of *The Sound of Music,* Maria leaves behind her convent life — which she had believed was her destiny — and becomes a wife and a mother to seven children. Over the course of the two-year tour, playing the part of Maria close to five hundred times, I began to feel the same way. I left behind my solitary career as a country music performer to become an accepted member in the family of Broadway performers. I later starred in the role of Anna in the Broadway production of *The King and I.* They have asked me "home" to do other shows many times over the past decade. I hope they keep the door open, because . . . someday.

STUFF

Seriously, the directions are in Chinese. Help!

Osmond Family Archive

"Sight unseen" was how my friend described her impulsive spring-cleaning technique.

She told me that she went into the storage area of her house, carried out three large dusty, taped-shut boxes, and put them into her car. She then dropped them off at the Children's Hospital thrift store as a donation.

"Wait!" I said in disbelief. "How do you know what you gave away if you never looked inside?"

"I don't," she answered. "It was really liberating. It's the new bra burning! I'm protesting being smothered by too much stuff."

Her enthusiasm was convincing.

"I hope you didn't accidentally give away any heirlooms," I said.

She assured me that she knew exactly where she had stored everything of personal value to herself and her family. She was guessing that the unopened boxes had contained all types of unnecessary things, from old Christmas decorations to coffee mugs, from toys long outgrown to high-fat cookbooks that were no longer useful.

"Probably full of ugly stationery, mismatched picture frames, outdated evening bags, and all of those things that had been packed up and stored in case I needed them someday."

As my friend summarized, "If 'someday' hasn't come up in the last two years, then somebody else could probably make better use of whatever is in the box."

Her new goal was to not use storage at all, except for extra sheets and blankets and maybe one box of tree lights and ornaments.

In America, where one in ten households pay for an off-site storage space, and over 1.8 billion square feet is being used to hold our personal belongings, doesn't it appear obvious that many of us have a "stuff" problem?

I hate to point fingers, but in my house it's mostly because of the kids. Really. I kept track for an entire week, so I have scientific proof.

I started on a Monday, and this is what entered my house via a person under four feet eight inches tall within eight and a half hours: a scouts manual and neck scarf; a thirty-two-ounce empty pineapple juice can that was supposed to be converted into a small hamburger grill as a project; four Happy Meal *Star Wars* toys with eight switches and buttons and bobbling heads; two empty nugget cartons; a box of sixty-four crayons along with twenty-four washable markers; two birthday goodie bags each containing seventeen loose plastic objects; a hammock pillow; a stack of permission slips from sports organizations; a crumpled ribbon of stickers; and book club order sheets. In addition to that, new sneakers, a fake tree branch for the real lizard, video game cartridges, football shoulder pads, a Razor scooter, and a combination lock were all unloaded from the car into the house. Two plastic lightsabers (borrowed from a playmate), a blow-up air mattress for sleepover pals, and a DVD of *SpongeBob SquarePants: Pest of the West* rounded out the accumulation of stuff we had acquired from eight a.m. to four thirty p.m. I think I missed the partridge in a pear tree.

I'd need a spreadsheet to give you the details of Tuesday through Sunday, but let me just say that 0.0001 percent of it belonged to me.

Truly, I can't seem to even acquire a much-needed new four-dollar spatula to flip the French toast after the last utensil was consumed by my rabidly efficient garbage disposal. After watching shards of silicone fly through the air, I now use an extension rod to turn the disposal on from across the room! It's so ferocious that the other day when my teenager's little black poodle went missing for a bit, we all turned to look suspiciously at the garbage disposal. We've nicknamed the disposal "Jaws."

Recently, I was in New York for a press junket and to appear on a number of morning shows. As the car that picked us up from the airport drove through the streets of Manhattan, I started to notice that an "organizational" or "container" store had sprung up on almost every city block — huge two-story shops that sell stuff to help us hold all of our stuff.

As we neared the hotel where we were staying, I asked my longtime manager, Karl, if he had much stuff put away in storage. He burst into laughter.

"I pay ninety dollars a month to store five sets of water skis we used twice in the mid-eighties, a saddle from a horse that passed away fifteen years ago, and a treadmill that was cutting-edge technology in 1996," Karl said, shaking his head. "And, if I'm not mistaken, we have the minibike we gave Brett for his twelfth birthday."

Brett is now in his thirties, married, with two sons.

"Brett probably doesn't even remember that bike," Karl said with a sigh. "I don't know why we still have it."

"How many years have you had the storage space?" I asked him.

"Twenty-eight," he replied, shaking his head. "That's over twenty-eight thousand dollars I've paid to store about three thousand dollars' worth of stuff."

We couldn't help but laugh. "Maybe Jimmy Hoffa's in there," I said.

As I looked at Karl's sweet, sentimental father face, I tried to remember what I had been given as a child, the possessions I thought were so necessary to my existence, which were now long forgotten. I still have a couple of baby dolls that were the very beginnings of my collection, but almost everything else has been shuffled out of my memory bank except, oddly enough, some purchases I made with only one penny.

On summer days in Huntsville, Utah, when I was a little girl, my mother would give me one penny to take to the corner store. Being in a small town, this tiny one-room shop was the "everything" store. There were two or three choices of laundry detergent on the same shelf as the boxed cake mixes. (Ever had a devil's food cake with a Dreft aftertaste?) Garden hose or panty hose, fishing waders or boxed stuffing mix, they were all available. Paper dolls, thumbtacks, canned fruit, and packs of bobby pins shared a display bin on a countertop. I had my personal favorite section of the store. On the end of one crowded aisle were bins of little toys like tiny plastic telephones, magnetic dolls that kissed, plastic jewelry, and water pistols. I would study each toy as if it were a museum piece, something to be hoped for in the future, but nothing I could have today just because I wanted it.

Above the toy section was a row of penny candy in jars, and I remember the distinct feeling of being lucky enough to have a penny to spend. It took quite a while to choose because I knew there was no second chance. One penny was all I had, and one piece was all I would get, even if I regretted my choice.

To this day, I couldn't tell you what shoes I wore to the Emmy Awards in 1999, or even what jewelry I wore on QVC last week, but I can remember exactly the look of a grape Pixy Stix, a red jawbreaker, and the line drawings of children playing that were imprinted on a Tootsie Roll wrapper. It wasn't how much I wanted the candy that keeps this memory ever present in my mind; it was the process of learning how to be selective. The power I felt as a child in choosing came from actually having to choose, and then in appreciating that I had figured out what I really wanted. I doubt that I would even recall this time of my life if I had been given a dollar every day.

As our next generation zigzags down the Short Attention Span Disposable speedways that our society seems to encourage, we're paying a lot of money to store away too much stuff that barely had any significance from the beginning.

I decided that it was time for a family project. I gave to each child a cardboard box with instructions to pack up the toys they hadn't played with in the past year. And if it was broken or missing pieces, they were to put it in a separate box. With some moaning and groaning, as if they had been asked to literally separate the wheat from the chaff, as in biblical times, they began to choose which possessions to box up and which ones they cherished.

I told them that I would clean out my own

cosmetics drawer and shelves next to my bathroom mirror. I had no idea how many products I had and never used until I started to sort them. I was preoccupied for so long that at one point my eleven-year-old rolled an orange through the door to me and said: "You better have a snack, Mom." Well, I was starting to feel weak.

By the end of the day, four cardboard boxes of toys had been sealed closed with packing tape and put in the car.

"Where will our toys be?" my nine-year-old asked.

"Probably in a lot of different homes all over this city," I answered. "Won't you feel good knowing that some boy or girl will play with them and appreciate them every single day?"

There was a momentary gasp and then slowly some secret smiles. I'm always touched by the joy my kids get from knowing they helped someone else. Their eyes sparkle and they always seem to stand a bit taller.

Brianna carried my box of unused cosmetics to the car. "Who is going to need all this makeup?" she asked dryly.

"I don't know, sweetheart. Maybe there's a clown school in town."

My twelve-year-old picked up the carton

of broken toys. "Where does all this junk go?"

I could have sworn I heard a rumbling sound, like an empty stomach. It came from the kitchen.

The kids looked at each other and my nine-year-old yelled, "It's Jaws!"

In Search of a Last Name

The brilliant Ray Bolger re-creating his Scarecrow, talented Paul Williams as the Cowardly Lion, and the wonderful Lucille Ball as TinWoman. Donny and I were the luckiest kids in showbiz.

Osmond Family Archive

Osmond Family Archive

"We're four people in search of a last name."

Cher said this line onstage while wearing a bright red sweater with a giant sequined *C* on the front. The *S, D,* and *M* occupying the sweaters next to her laughed along.

This was before Madonna came on the music scene and long before the introductions of Usher, Shakira, or Jewel. At that time, hardly any performers were recognized on a first-name basis only.

Donny and I were the *D* and *M,* appearing as guests on *The Sonny and Cher Show* in 1976. A couple of months before, they had appeared on our show. Every variety show before Sonny and Cher's and ours had used full names in the titles: *The Red Skelton Show, The Andy Williams Show, The Carol Burnett Show,* to name a few. I guess Sid and Marty Krofft, who produced our original show, thought "Donny and Marie Osmond" sounded like a married couple. The brother-sister thing seemed obvious to us, but when our talk show aired twenty-two years later, there were *still* people who thought we were husband and wife. That's just gross, okay?

Sonny and Cher had been through a very public divorce the year before. They had each tried to launch separate variety shows, but it seemed that no one wanted to think of them as unhappy and apart, and so they joined forces once again for a new show. As Sonny reminded the audience: "Together, but no longer related."

We had been invited on to sing a silly love song. Literally. The four of us stood side by side to sing Paul McCartney's number-one hit on the Billboard charts, "Silly Love Songs." Supposedly, Paul wrote this song in response to the music critics calling his music lightweight. I don't think he expected it to zoom up the charts, but that was what people were into then. People loved the song. The Vietnam War had ended the year before and people were looking for light-hearted entertainment. Their mood rings were blue, they adopted pet rocks, I guess to prove that everything deserved love, and even a simple yellow smiley face T-shirt was a best seller. It's probably why the Sonny and Cher producers wanted Donny and me to come on the show. The deepest issue we were bringing to public awareness at that time was our different tastes in music. Me: country. Him: rock 'n' roll.

Donny and Sonny stood between Cher and me, but a lot of other factors seemed to separate us, as well.

By age seventeen, Cher had already begun her serious relationship with Sonny; at sixteen, I wasn't even allowed to date. Cher's singing voice is deep and rich; mine was sweet and high. She had gorgeous, thick, waist-long hair; I wore a wispy, chin-length pageboy. We ice-skated on our show; Cher skated over anything Sonny had to say with a hysterically funny cool glance and a sharp tongue. Cher had exotic, captivating features; mine were extremely "teenager." Even though Cher and I both had the famous Bob Mackie design our wardrobes for the show, the results were as far apart as could be possible. Cher's costumes were bold and daring for that time, even exposing her navel; mine were much more modest, barely exposing my neckline. Looking back, Bob probably was able to create my outfits from the yards and yards of material he had left over after making Cher's! I felt like the ugly duckling. Cher always made a splash, no matter what she did. I thought I was going to drown in my awkwardness.

I was starting to constantly feel like a girl who was way out of her league. Standing onstage next to Raquel Welch and comparing my appearance to hers was enough to send me into a "hating myself" tailspin. It was pretty hard to leave my dressing room feeling like anything other than a poser playing dress up. As *Donny and Marie* became a hit on ABC, the most stunningly beautiful women celebrities of the day signed on for guest-star spots on our show. Among the many were Farrah Fawcett, Barbara Eden, Tina Turner, Jaclyn Smith, Cher . . . and two other gorgeous Chers who seemed to have it all: Cheryl Ladd and Cheryl Tiegs.

I wanted so much to be in my twenties and thirties, thinking that it would finally be the time when I didn't feel shy and self-conscious as a gawky-looking teenager.

When men tell me now that I was their first crush, it makes me smile. I have always been surprised that anyone even gave me a second glance, especially since Farrah Fawcett's famous red bathing suit poster had most young men walking around in a hypnotic trance that they didn't shake off until the 1980s.

Knowing that feathery blond hair and a red bathing suit would never be me, I was completely open to absorbing advice from that most famous redhead with the one-word name: Lucy. She appeared as a guest on our show in 1977. She was sixty-six years old, had starred in three television shows of her own, won multiple Emmy Awards, had great roles in movies, and was the first female owner of a large Hollywood production studio (Desilu). Beyond that, she was a comic Einstein, recognized around the world. She shattered the stereotype that women couldn't be the central character in a show, and proved that they could be both beautiful and brilliantly funny. She changed the scope of what was possible for women in entertainment forever.

I wasn't envious of her; I was terrified! She was a force of nature.

She walked onto the set of the *Donny and Marie* show as if she did it every day. She gave directions to everyone from the director to the seamstress to the sound engineer and the security guard at the stage door. Perhaps she stepped on the toes of some, but she never asked for time or effort from anyone that she didn't put into the show herself.

What I learned from Lucy in that brief rehearsal week has been useful for my entire career, including some practical advice that

I apply to almost every interview with every camera crew.

"Let me show you something, kiddo," she said to me the day before we taped the show. She grabbed a mirror from the back-stage makeup table and handed it to me.

She tugged on my elbow, walking me out to the center of our stage.

"As a woman, never allow this if you want to last in this business!"

I was worried that she was going to want to rewrite part of the script, but that wasn't her intention.

She tilted my face up toward the stage lights hung up high over our heads.

"Look in the mirror. This is very unattractive lighting for the female face," Lucy told me. "The light is too high. It gives women dark circles under their eyes and exaggerates the jowls."

She pointed out the results to me on her own face.

"Now watch!" she said, asking the crew to lower some of the lights to more of a straight-on position.

The results really were effective. The light was caught up in her eyes instead of under her eyes. Her whole face looked more lively and expressive.

Then she jostled me toward the camera.

"See how this lens is lower than my face?" she asked me. "This is a horrible angle for a woman. It creates a double chin, I don't care how young you are. You look awful. The camera is forgiving of men, but never of women. Got it?"

I did get it. I was taking a crash course in Lucille Ball entertainment wisdom and I knew that the lessons were ones I would use my entire career.

It seemed that Lucy knew how to make everything look better. On the morning of the taping, I came in early to have my hair done. Lucy was having her hair braided into numerous small braids. The hairstylist then pulled them tightly toward the back of her head and pinned them down, and put her wig on top. The effect of the braids being pulled back gave her a very natural-looking face-lift. I'm sure it was somewhat painful, but the results were pretty amazing.

Though I've yet to try her braiding trick for erasing the years, I have applied Lucy's other techniques whenever and wherever I can. Some camera crews, especially in Los Angeles, New York, and Utah, know what to expect now and are ready with beautiful lighting when I arrive. This past June, I was taping an interview for the American Heart Association. When I arrived on the set that day, I was greeted by one of the technicians, a guy I'd worked with several times before, with a good-hearted nature.

"We're all ready for you," he said, smiling, leading me to the chair in front of the camera. "Check out the Lucille Ball lighting. Pretty good, right?"

It was good, and much appreciated. After all, as Lucy taught me, there is no harm in giving yourself the best advantage whenever it's possible. And it's a lot more productive than worrying about aging.

It didn't seem that Lucy wasted any time wishing she could change anything that was out of her control. She worked with what she had and she turned it into genius. It was through Lucy that I learned early on that the way you feel about yourself at sixteen will be the way you feel at thirty and even forty, especially if you waste time always comparing yourself to others.

My initial fear of Lucy turned into a deep admiration when I understood the reason she didn't worry about what Donny or I or anyone else working on the show personally thought of her. She focused on only one thing: that she did her job well. She was there to entertain the audience in the studio and the millions of viewers at home. After all, that's supposedly the reason all performers get into the business. Isn't it? Though Donny and I may have been too young at the time to fully appreciate being exposed to the committed work ethic of stars like Bob Hope, Sammy Davis, Jr., Paul Lynde, John Wayne, Andy Williams, Milton Berle, and even Groucho Marx, we know that those early lessons have definitely contributed to our long successful careers.

As I was preparing my *Magic of Christmas* holiday tour for 2007, I crossed paths with Cher at . . . of all places . . . a famous costume designer's studio in Los Angeles. It was the same one where we used to see each other in the seventies, while having our Bob Mackie fittings. This time, Cher was getting ready to open her new show at Caesars Palace in Vegas, and I would soon be going through the same process for our show at the Flamingo.

Even in jeans and boots, Cher looked amazing as ever, in great physical shape, toned, and radiant. Probably because I was dressed in my dancing warm-ups, a T-shirt and one of my haphazard ponytails, I thought about my teenage insecurities during my appearance on *The Sonny and Cher Show*. Time certainly is the great equalizer. Those differences that seemed like the great divide between us at that time have narrowed and filled in with many similar life experiences: parenting, divorce, loss, charity work, and the challenges of re-creating ourselves as entertainers again and again.

I was smiling while reading the list of entertainers performing in Las Vegas this year: Cher, Bette Midler, Barry Manilow, Neil Sedaka, the Osmond Brothers, Paul Anka, Louie Anderson, George Wallace, the Smothers Brothers, and Donny and Marie. It's like Vegas hiccupped and the seventies came back up! It seems that, once again, especially with all the troubles going on in the world, people are craving lighthearted entertainment, a time to set aside worries for a while and just enjoy. It makes me happy that my career has now lasted as long as Lucy's. I know it's a combination of blessings, hard work, and the tilt of the spotlight that has kept the sparkle in my eyes. Oh, and the audience. *Always* the audience.

DUDE, IT'S FOR ME

One more *"in-terminal-able"* travel layover for my road warrior kids and me.

Osmond Family Archive

My teenagers love to listen to Joni Mitchell — not the latest release, but Joni from 1971, her *Blue* album. I understand why. The music was written during a year that Joni took off from her rising career to travel the world, to write and paint. That lifestyle has always appealed to teenagers — well, to all of us, really, don't you think?

All of my children love to travel and have a blast living on a tour bus, especially when I took my *Magic of Christmas* holiday show on the road in 2006 and 2007. This was the first road tour for my four younger children. They had never known Mommy as a stage singer and performer. They only knew me to work as a radio show host and doll designer on QVC. My older kids had shown them many of the original *Donny and Marie* shows on tape, but I don't think they could make the leap right away that the teenager they were watching then is Mommy now.

When our family chats it up about good times, my children's best memories are never about the sights, landmarks, museums, or other remarkable places we visit while on the road. Their best memories are most often about something that happened while we were on the tour bus; really delightful things like being stranded in a sleet storm in Wisconsin, sharing truck stop nachos with cheese so unnatural it glows in the dark, or being catapulted out of the top bunk during a sharp U-turn and plummeting to the floor. Isn't it interesting how your concept of fun changes after age twenty-one? Suddenly a trip to the emergency room isn't such a laugh fest. However, getting off the bus with an undiscovered banana peel stuck to your tush will always be funny. Or is that just me?

Living on a tour bus can be very liberating, once you adjust to the minimal lifestyle. It's rather freeing to temporarily shed all the distractions that come with an entire house and its contents. My own memories of the kids traveling with me by bus are some of my favorites as well.

When I was touring the country music circuit in the early nineties, playing every honky-tonk, festival, and fair on the planet, my second son, Michael, was only a baby, and the older three children were under age seven. We had to leave Nashville very early in the morning to arrive at the destination city by early afternoon for the first concert. My kids, still in their footed pj's, would get on the couch of the bus and watch out of the window until we approached the Krispy Kreme store. Then they would jump up and down excitedly seeing the red "Hot Doughnuts Now" sign lit up, knowing that they would be fresh from the fryer. Warm glazed doughnuts became our traditional "leaving town" food on every country music tour. Their enthusiasm in anticipating a warm doughnut was adorable. Well, it was cute coming from little kids. When the other musicians and I started jumping up and down from excitement the bus driver would shout back to us: "Stop! You're stressing the shock absorbers." And by the end of the tour, after many, many Krispy Kreme mornings, it wasn't just the jumping that was stressing the struts; it was the shocking number of extra pounds all of us had gained thanks to those glazed morsels. It was like we had picked up a couple of additional band members along the way!!

My children have always been exposed to a wide variety of music, from country to classical, metal to Broadway musicals. Even my younger kids have very eclectic tastes: Matthew listens to and sings Elvis songs; Abigail grooves out to Annie Lennox; and Brianna has the funk down. One day Brandon wanted to hear a Tom Jones CD he discovered in our collection, so I played it during dinnertime.

After studying the song list and then the cover of the CD, Rachael said, "He can really sing. So, why was he on the *Brady Bunch*?"

I guess that dark, short, curly 1970s hair could only mean one thing: the *Brady Bunch* dad.

I told them about Tom Jones and how I had appeared on his TV show, and even recorded a duet with him. Then we all jumped to our feet to dance to "It's Not Unusual" and "What's New, Pussycat?"

Some entertainers — people like Joni Mitchell, Elvis, and even Tom Jones — will always be relatable to others beyond their own generation. I still love almost any Loretta Lynn song, and there's no one like Gladys Knight. Her recording of "Neither One of Us (Wants to Be the First to Say Good-bye)" surpasses generational boundaries because the theme is universal: when relationships go stale, saying good-bye is heartbreaking. The originality of the Pips' backup dancing has transcended time, too, right into the Osmond Brothers' dance steps in the seventies, and on into the glittering nineties with groups like Destiny's Child.

It's fun for me now to see more and more teenagers and young people in the audience of our Vegas show at the Flamingo. Some of them only know me as a doll designer or as a contestant on *Dancing with the Stars,* and Donny as an *Entertainment Tonight* correspondent. Often, someone under age fifteen will say to me after a show, "Wow, I was totally shocked that you can sing, too."

Okay, so maybe "Morning Side of the Mountain" and "Deep Purple" haven't dominated current playlists. If the teenagers only know me from the television work I've done in the last five years, that's all right. As long as they don't look at me and say, "She can really sing. So why did she play Joanie on *Happy Days?*"

One woman brought her teenaged daughter to the "meet and greet" after the show. She coaxed her daughter to tell me her first Osmond experience.

The girl turned bright red.

"It's no big deal," she said. "When your talk show was on, I was only three. I couldn't really pronounce *Donny and Marie.*"

This is where the mom jumped in.

"She used to say, 'I want to watch diarrhea!' "

"That's both your names smushed together." The teenager shrugged, with a grin.

"Smushed? Okay, enough with the diarrhea references," I said and laughed.

"Sorry," she said. "But I really did like the show. I never wanted to miss it."

"It's okay," I said, putting my arm around the girl's shoulders. "Donny and Marie. Diarrhea. Either way, it kept you close to home. And that's good."

I've always expected to have some teenage girls as fans, because quite a few of them are doll collectors, too. Once in a while, though, I'm surprised by who wants to meet me.

I was having a quick salad with a friend in a restaurant and two boys came up to the table to ask for an autograph. They were wearing hip, skateboarder clothes, leather bracelets, and sneakers with skulls on them, and had long sweeping bangs covering their eyes.

I asked the first young man if the autograph was for his mom.

"Dude, it's for me. I used to watch the

talk show you did with Donny when I was little. Me and my mom."

Mind you, he was "little" in 2000.

The other boy handed me a paper on which was drawn a heart with an arrow through it and asked me to sign inside of the heart.

"Ah. You like older women?" I said only to tease him.

"Yeah," he said. "You're single, right?"

At this point I looked up at the boy, who raised his eyebrows at me.

I wanted to burst out laughing and say something like, "My name is not Mrs. Robinson," but I was already surprised he knew me at all; I didn't think I could push the point of reference back to 1967.

Instead, I thought I'd play along.

"I am single. And I like going to the movies."

He looked a bit stunned at my straight-faced answer and then he said sincerely, "Okay, but you'll have to drive, cuz I'm only fourteen. Almost fifteen!"

"Well," I told him, handing him the autograph, "in my day, the dudes paid for the date."

"That's gonna take me a while, then," he said with some dejection. "Too bad. Cuz you're a babe."

"No, *you're* the babe," I said, laughing. Though I meant it absolutely literally.

I had to be at least a little flattered. Mostly, I loved knowing that their happy memories of watching the talk show with their families is what propelled them to ask for my autograph.

Like music, it seems that television shows can transcend time, especially if they are part of a good memory of watching them with family or friends. It's similar to the tour bus experience. You're all in the same room, anticipating something fun, and heading to the same destination: entertainment.

Because of television (our show was dubbed into seventeen languages) our audiences in Vegas come from all around the globe. They have happy memories of Friday nights watching *Donny and Marie* with their families and friends, and they want to share that with their own kids.

I'm grateful that they enjoy the Vegas show, but I also know that their pleasure goes deeper than seeing Donny and me. They are there to get a certain feeling back, if only for an hour or two. Even if they are forty-something, almost fifty, their spirits are still "fourteen, almost fifteen."

I think it's a lot like the way my kids and I still have a hard time passing up a Krispy Kreme store when we see the "Hot Doughnuts Now" sign lit up. It's not because of the doughnuts anymore. It's more about recapturing happy memories of feeling safe and loved and together. If any show I did, in the forty-plus years of my career, made other people feel something similar, then all I can say is: "Dude, that's pretty cool."

WE WANT YOU AROUND

Eight years to put the extra weight on . . .

. . . and only four months to take it off, thanks to NutriSystem.

Whenever I felt self-conscious about weight gain, I would always excuse my insecurities by saying, "Who cares? It is what it is. I'm happy."

It was true. I wasn't *unhappy* about my forty extra pounds, but I always had to end the statement right after the word "happy," because adding anything else would be a lie. What was I going to say? "I'm happy to have to unzip my jeans every time I sit down"? Or: "I'm happy that I'm four sizes bigger than I used to be"? Or: "I'm happy that I can't sleep at night because my knees ache from carrying around so many extra pounds"? The whole truth was that I no longer felt comfortable in my skin.

I turned forty years old in 1999 and I think I celebrated that milestone by starting to gain one pound for every year of my life! Somehow, an unnoticed five pounds each year after age forty made its way to my middle and stayed, even though it was getting pretty crowded! The pounds that couldn't squeeze onto my stomach just moved around to my back. It was crafty of them. Out of sight, out of mind.

Even when I had to admit to being a size ten — really a size twelve, which isn't good for a size-four frame — I still kept up the internal dialogue that it was only some "water weight" from the salt on the popcorn, or from flying the red-eye from LA to New York. As most third-graders know, a gallon of water weighs eight pounds, yet I managed to convince my brain that I was carrying five extra gallons of water. You know, I was just like a camel. The fact is a camel's hump is made of fat, and so was mine! However, many women are like camels in that we can take extreme heat in any situation and still keep going. We have to.

The women I know are superb at crisis management. Like most of the women I know, I feel like I do aerobics all day long because I hit the floor running the moment the alarm goes off in the morning.

One of my girlfriends sent me an early-morning e-mail with the subject line "This has to be fiction!" The link was to a blog by a woman describing the start of her day with phrases like: "contemplated the stillness," "loved these moments of peace and quiet as I gazed at my daily list," and "felt the serenity of the morning dew."

Now, there's a bunch of doo if I ever heard it.

I saw my friend an hour later in the same place where we catch up for thirty seconds every weekday, the drop-off lane in front of the grade school. She was trying to apply some mascara in the rearview mirror as her kids unloaded their backpacks and sports equipment from the car.

"Hey!" I called out to her as I wrestled the knot out of the back of Abby's hair, using my finger nails as a comb. "Thanks for the laugh! I have to run this morning and 'contemplate the stillness' of taking my teenager for his driving permit, and then pick up three prescriptions and hurry into the studio to set the sound levels on the song I recorded at midnight last night."

"Oh. A slow morning, then?" she said. "If you have time to chat, I'll be 'gazing' at six loads of laundry, and enjoying having to pry the 'piece' of gum my four-year-old stuck in the DVD player!"

"Have fun!" I waved, folding a last-minute permission slip into a paper airplane and sailing it serenely out the passenger door to my eight-year-old.

As I drove away, I called out to her: "By the way, you have the hose to a gas pump hanging from the side of your car. Love ya!"

The reality for most women I know is that we take care of our kids, spouses, parents, brothers, coworkers, neighbors, community, and brothers. (Did I say that already? Well, mine can be exhausting.) We take care of every*body* else, but rarely take the time to care for our own bodies.

Unintentionally, we proclaim our manic lives like a greeting between friends.

"Hey, how are you? Would love to chat, but I'm so stressed."

There's a silent agreement that the most stressed mama wins!! But really, she loses out on a lot more in the long run. Especially when, like me, there is a history of cardio-vascular disease in the family.

When my mother had her first massive stroke, I wanted to be with her as much as I could. I would take care of my business obligations during the day, take care of the kids in the evening, and then take care of my mother through the night. I was getting eight hours of sleep . . . per week!

To energize myself I would get large milk-shakes from the hospital cafeteria almost nightly. Ice cream is a wonderful medicine

— just ask Dr. Baskin or Dr. Robbins or Dr. Dazs, as in Häagen. This probably wouldn't have had a huge effect on my weight except that because I didn't have time to eat all day, I would grab a cheeseburger and fries or taquitos with guacamole or even an ice-cream cone with guacamole on the way to the hospital. There's nothing like combining your five servings of fruit with your three servings of dairy in four servings of ice cream! I was starting to look like the food pyramid with legs.

One early, early morning about a month into my mother's hospital stay, as I was leaning over to kiss her good-bye for the day, she whispered to me, "Marie, don't do what I did. Take care of yourself."

As positive as my mom's attitude always was, she could tell that her chances of recovery had now narrowed, mostly because she never made herself a priority. She was too busy to ever put herself first. Besides helping to take care of my father and both sets of my grandparents, there were the nine of us children that she wanted to be certain were cared for well. She also did hours and hours of charity work and maintained five-page newsletters to family, friends, and fans. I guarantee that when it came to responding to other people, the words "deal with it yourself" never crossed my mom's lips.

Following her second stroke at age seventy-seven, she slowly declined over twelve months to the point of being almost immobilized. It was incredibly tough to see my mother's youthful spirit trapped in a worn-out body. Her youthful sense of humor, however, never declined.

After my dad moved my mother home to make her remaining time more enjoyable, day nurses would come to help with medications, breathing equipment, and IVs. In attempting to move her from the bed to a chair one day, the day-care person and my mother both lost their balance and toppled over on the carpeted floor. My father and a close family friend heard the soft thud and hurried into her bedroom. Seeing my mother lying on the floor, unhurt, but with her head halfway under the bed, they asked, "What are you doing?"

The day nurse was about in tears over the incident. My mother, always the caretaker, said, "We're just looking for quarters."

The nurses would duke it out between them to be the one who got to come to my parents' condo to take care of my mother. One of them explained, "We take care of people who aren't nearly as bad off as your mom, but who are so negative. Your mother is so appreciative over any little thing we do for her. She always says thank you, she always makes us laugh, and she always asks about our families."

That's how my sweet mother was, even in the final weeks of her life, never putting herself first.

A hospice nurse once told me that when a patient passes on, there is a strong sense that the spirit of the person stays near their body, though not in it, for at least a little while.

The morning my mother passed away, on Mother's Day of 2004, I could feel her spirit there in the room. As the medical people began to roll away the monitors and remove the respirator, it was as though my mother stood next to me, thanking her body for being so good to her, carrying her through seventy-nine years of living. It had a profound effect on me. I so often ignore that a woman's body is not only a miracle because it can give birth, but because it is so resilient. The body never gives up on us . . . it will do anything to keep the heart beating, but we so often neglect it.

My mother's words, "Take care of yourself," resided in my memory, but I still didn't take the time to take them to heart. That is, until my heart was affected, both physically and emotionally.

One November afternoon, I was rehearsing my 2006 *Magic of Christmas* tour with the band. We were going through the opening number, "We Need a Little Christmas." The choreography involved moving at an energetic pace across the stage, lighting up Christmas trees as I went with the wave of my arm. I guess that was the magic part!! David Copperfield, I'm not.

By the time I got through the song and to the other side of the stage it was obvious to me that I was "hauling out" a lot more than the holly. I was hauling around a kindergartner. After all, forty pounds is the weight of the average five-year-old. I came off the side of the stage huffing and puffing like the Big Bad Wolf but without enough breath to blow anything down.

My oldest son, Stephen, handed me a bottle of water.

I tried to make light of my breathlessness, though it was frightening me.

"I need more than a little Christmas. I need a little oxygen!!"

He wasn't laughing. He had something to tell me. He had been elected by the rest of my children to give me a message.

"Mom," he said, "we think you're beautiful no matter what you weigh, but we want

320

you to start taking care of yourself."

I tried to calm his worries. "Sweetheart, I'll be fine."

He continued. "You don't understand. We need you. We want you to be around for us and for our kids, too. Please, Mom. What would we do without you?"

The band started to cue up to rehearse the "Christmas Waltz," but I couldn't go onstage to sing because tears choked my throat. I understood exactly what my son was telling me, even though I wanted to deck him down a size or two!

I understood because I still wanted my mom around. I wanted her to be there for my kids. I wanted to talk to her about my disintegrating marriage, my concerns for my teenagers, and how to help my little kids cope. I wanted to share with her the new stupid joke of the day, my new line of crafts and fabric, have our scriptural discussions that I loved so much, and every other thing big and small that only a mother and daughter can do together. I've always wanted to follow in her footsteps and become a happy grandma. But in the area of self-care I was still ignoring her strong plea that I must take a path different from hers.

My mother believed, as I do, that if you can't change your circumstances, you always have the option of changing your attitude. In this case, I could still change my circumstances, but I knew I had to change my attitude first.

If I didn't feel an urgency to do something for myself, I needed to do it for my children. Abby was only in preschool. At age forty-seven, I was still missing my mom; why was I risking leaving my own daughter when she was only four? I had to make the time to put my health first.

Still, in the beginning, I had no idea how I would find the time to make it happen. I couldn't carve out an extra hour in my day; it just wasn't there. I didn't have time to buy a juicer and peel vegetables. When I asked people about dieting, they would make suggestions like counting points, going to a weight-loss group, or taking herbal appetite suppressants or even medication. I didn't want side effects, or to have someone watch me step on scales. Like most women I know, it wasn't about laziness — it was about busy-ness. We eat for energy. Dieting has always made me feel too tired.

I needed an answer to show up at my door. And amazingly, it did. After looking over weight-loss options on the Internet and doing some research on several of the top weight-loss programs, I decided to go with

NutriSystem, mostly because it was easy and healthy. I loved that I didn't have to think about measuring portion sizes. I like food too much to constantly analyze it. I knew I wasn't going to stick to any diet if I had to process the process. With NutriSystem, I could just grab and go. For me, it's like buying shoes. I love shoes, but if you made me pick out the parts — the insole, the upper, the heel, the leather — I'd just try to find something else that I liked to do.

NutriSystem set the portion sizes, packaged the food, and checked the nutritional value, so all I had to do was order what I liked, pick up my delivery from my front porch, and stock my shelves. It's real food, like lasagna, and bean and rice soup, and macaroni and cheese, so I didn't have to decipher ingredients or try to trick my taste buds with substitutions. Please! I'm not a woman who wants to pretend that rolled oats are cheese. With NutriSystem the oatmeal is the oatmeal and the lasagna is actual lasagna! And I could be real about what I could handle. The only real effort I ever had to make was ordering a drive-thru garden salad. That was tough! There was no going cold turkey on anything, including sweets. Caramel popcorn and the chocolate crunch bars got me through without one minute of crabby withdrawal from milkshakes, and the NutriSystem ice-cream sandwiches are not only my favorite treat, but my kids' as well. The most significant thing I learned from the NutriSystem program was the necessity of eating three meals a day. My body responded very quickly to this healthy consistency. Over the years of irregular eating patterns I had thrown my metabolism into famine mode. No wonder my body would hold onto any calorie I consumed.

In an unexpected way, I felt better and better every day, in addition to losing an average of a pound or two each week. My energy balanced out because I wasn't swinging wildly between starving myself and then consuming whatever was on hand, from a half-eaten candy bar to the leftovers of my kids' peanut butter toast and blueberry pancakes. I could step into the pantry in the morning and put one or two NutriSystem meals or snacks right into my bag and head out.

My mom loved good, memorable quotes and used to write them into her newsletters. One was from Ralph Waldo Emerson: "Once you make a decision, the universe conspires to make it happen." I think that one has stayed around since the 1800s because everyone who tries the advice finds it to be true after a little while. In this century, it's referred to as quantum physics. I'd just call it being positive.

Three weeks into my NutriSystem program, I had lost about six pounds. It was a miraculous mood booster, especially because my knees hurt less with each melting pound. Once I started to feel a little lighter on my feet I wanted to start toning up, too.

To start off, I'd take brisk walks with the kids, which had a double benefit. Of course it was aerobic, and without the distraction of video games and cell phones and TV, it was also a great way to really get to hear about what was going on in their lives. One of my favorite activities is reading, but I had to find a way to make it active. So instead of sitting on the couch, I bought an iPod and began to download audio books to listen to as I walked while the kids were in school.

Then one afternoon, the call came in from my manager, Karl. ABC wanted to have me on season five of *Dancing with the Stars*. It gave me pause — really big "deer in the headlights" pause. Only a few months before, I was losing my breath with a wave of my arm onstage. Was I really going to have the courage to ballroom dance on live national television?

My children were my biggest cheerleaders.

Stephen said to me, "It'll be like having a personal trainer work with you every day and you'll get paid for it. Why would you say no to that?"

I ran the idea by three girlfriend coworkers the next day during a doll design meeting.

One of them said to me, "Well, you used to dance on the original *Donny and Marie* show, right?"

"Not like this!" I answered. "Besides, we didn't really dance, we more or less just grooved to the beat and pointed."

"They'll probably have celebrities on there that are ten or twenty years younger than you," another added. "I'd hate to compete with that. What if there's a model?!"

We all gasped! Of *course* they would bring in a model. It's tele-*vision.*

"And the costumes!" I responded. "Between the low cuts and the high cuts, I'll look like a cut of pork roast."

We all shuddered at the possibilities.

The most practical friend in the group sorted out the options: "Look at it this way. You have no time. You're getting divorced. You've got eight kids and you're already crazy busy. You're in your midforties and, even though you're dropping a few pounds, the costumes can be revealing and you're still overweight. I think the answer is perfectly clear. Right?"

A hush fell over all of us sitting at the table.

"You're right," I said. After a long minute of consoling looks from around the table, I stood up. "I'm going to do it."

They all looked stunned. But it only took a moment for them to understand, as only the truest of girlfriends do, that sometimes you've got to prove to yourself that you can still take on a challenge, even against all of the odds.

Almost in unison, all three of them said, "Go for it."

I did. And the universe conspired to make it happen!

IT'S ONLY SAND

Well, photographer Richard Avedon once told me that I have an "Audrey Hepburn neck," but this is extreme!

Osmond Family Archive

Somewhere inside this block of clay had to be my face. I made a promise to my doll collectors that in 2008 I would sculpt myself as a baby. It was a promise I wanted to break.

As I looked at my creation on the table in front of me, I thought, "Self-portraits should be left to brilliant artists like Frida Kahlo." Or I could call this doll "Baby Frida" instead of "Baby Olive Marie," because so far I'd sculpted one long brow that went from ear to ear. If I stopped using tweezers for several months, this had a chance of resembling me someday, but not me as a baby.

I used the water in a china saucer from one of my mother's favorite holiday pattern collections to dampen my clay-covered fingers, and smoothed over the forehead area, again, for the seventh time.

The delicate poinsettia pattern on the

inside edge of the china became coated with a gray-colored paste within seconds. I'm certain I could have found an old yogurt container or put the water in a plastic bowl, something with no sentimental value. But I chose this particular china saucer. It helped me channel happy memories of childhood. My mother would have approved. She was never overly delicate with her collectibles, including her china.

I had set up a doll-sculpting area in my house, covering the carpeting, tabletops, walls, and chairs with plastic sheeting, yards and yards of it.

One lesson I learned quickly, after the first time I ever sculpted a doll, is this: The clay that is used to sculpt heads really has legs! It can travel. Far! I've had a waffle come out of the toaster a week later with clay dust stuck to it.

I considered leaving the plastic up permanently, even after I finished sculpting. With four children under age twelve, two teenagers at home, and an ever-expanding animal kingdom, it would be a real timesaver when it came to cleaning the house. I could just hose off the sheets of plastic. I wouldn't be the first Osmond to live that way.

My grandparents on my father's side

covered every fabric object in their house with plastic slipcovers, from the lamp shades to the ottomans. There was nothing quite like a Saran Wrap snooze on grandma's couch. On hot summer days, when your skin adhered to the plastic, or pools of sweat gathered under your kneecaps, it would take a minimum of two other family members to get you pried up off the sofa. For my grandparents, comfort was secondary. The plastic was a mental health choice. They could wipe down the house after the grandkids left and still have furniture that looked brand-new.

My grandmother might have needed crisis counseling if she saw me using my mother's china for a mini-sink; but using it helps me feel my mother's presence. She loved my dolls, and she believed that you should use and appreciate those things that bring you joy.

When my brothers and I were growing up, there were many, many meals shared on this china. At least once a week, usually on family night, we would set the table with her best glassware and real silverware. It was Mother's way of teaching us what was important — give to those whom you love most the best that you have to offer. Possessions are never more important than people.

It was a lesson my mother learned at a

young age from her own grandmother. She passed along to me a story of when she was a little girl and she dropped and broke a china plate from her grandmother's collection. Frightened that she would be in trouble, my mother approached her grandmother and, with tears in her eyes, asked forgiveness. She remembered distinctly the impression it left on her when her grandmother dried her eyes and said: "Toss it out, Olive. It's only sand."

The china was obviously beautifully refined and expensive sand, yet I think that my great-grandmother had it right in the big picture. After all, a diamond is only some highly organized carbon; cashmere once grazed on a plateau and bleated; a pearl is the result of a splinter in the backside of an oyster . . . and the most beautiful porcelain doll started out as a block of clay.

My mother was the one who started me on collecting dolls. She was so very happy, after giving birth to seven boys in a row, to finally have a daughter to dress in pink and load up with beautiful dolls. Sharing a household with nine men, I think my mom and I would have collected anything that had its mouth sealed shut!

It was the perfect hobby, especially while touring the world as a child. There is a universal quality to dolls no matter what the language or the culture. My mother and I would explore each new location by starting out in a doll shop. It didn't matter if we were in Malaysia, Japan, Sweden, or Mexico, we could find some common ground with strangers through dolls. After all, dolls have been around as long as there have been children. Archaeologists uncovered dolls in ancient Egyptian tombs that have held up for three thousand years. (One doll was found in a well-preserved lattice armchair, with a plastic slipcover on it. Kidding!)

I have to wonder if the little Egyptian girls took a sharp stone to the flax hair on their dolls and cut it all off into an uneven style, like I did with scissors to my first Barbie. My daughters all gave at least one radical haircut to a new doll at some point in their preschool lives. Jessica went for the ever-attractive mullet look on her baby doll, and Rachael's doll was graced with a spiked punk rocker do. Brianna liked the clean, close crew-cut look, and at age three, she did her own hair to match. The top of her little head had about one quarter inch of hair left. The sides were still long. She had to wear a comb-over style, held in place with a barrette, for months on end. Abby has always gone for the bald-headed dolls from the start. She would color the hair on with Magic Markers — her very own version of Nice 'n Easy for dolls.

More times than I can count, women will stop me in the airport, a store, or at an autograph signing to tell me: "I had the Donny and Marie Barbie dolls when I was growing up!!"

Then they get a sheepish look on their faces and add, "I cut all your hair off."

Most often they tell me that they cut the Marie doll's hair off when I went to a short style in between seasons of the show. Sometimes they tell me that they cut it into a pixie; others chose the ever-popular bi-level style, and a few have admitted to giving me a flattop. It's okay. I don't take it personally. They would have cut Donny's hair, too, except it was only molded plastic.

Donny and I were the very first celebrity Barbie dolls. My mother had traveled to New York City in 1975 with Jimmy, who was being sought after to star in a Broadway show. When she realized that Mattel was doing a trade show the same day as her meeting with producers, she decided to stop in and look at all of the dolls new to the market. At the Barbie booth, she scanned all of the various dolls and then suggested that they make "Donny and Marie" dolls by

336

using the same bodies and changing out the heads. (Leave it to a practical mother of nine.) The Mattel executives jumped on the idea. It was a big seller for them.

As a mother myself, and also as a woman, I appreciate that my mother asked that my doll be given the "Francie" body, instead of Barbie's. Francie was Barbie's "modern cousin." She had a more realistic figure. It would have been pretty uncomfortable to be a sixteen-year-old girl whose doll had a body like the original Barbie.

My Marie Osmond Collectible Porcelain Doll line was as great a source of joy for my mother as it has been for me. She would watch every one of my QVC shows whenever she could and give me ideas for new series, costumes, and hairstyles.

She and my daughter Rachael would watch the other doll and teddy bear shows on QVC to keep me posted about what was hot and what was not. It was good market research for each of their age groups. Having a great eye for design just like her grandma, even as a young girl Rachael could always pick out a terrific idea and spot the flaws in the ones that would never fly.

One afternoon, when Rachael was about eleven, I came home to find her watching a teddy bear show on QVC.

"Hey, Mom," she said, as I walked through to the kitchen. "They're selling a bear on here that's dressed in a fur coat."

"Do you like it?" I asked her.

"No! It's gross. Think about it, Mom. It would be like you wearing Uncle Donny."

She had a point. (Although I've never thought of Donny as being warm and fuzzy!)

I almost always showed my mother the new line of dolls I was designing, and if her face lit up, I felt like I had succeeded. The first face I ever sculpted was my mother's, as a tribute to her enthusiasm for dolls. I presented her doll, "Olive May," on a midnight QVC show in 1995. I began describing the doll and what my mother meant to me. I was anxious about how my debut sculpt would be received by collectors, so when the QVC producers started waving at me furiously two minutes into the show I thought it was a disaster. I tried to show more of the careful details I had added to this doll, from the ribbon ruffle along the collar of her blue satin dress to the beauty mark by her eye, a trademark of every doll I personally sculpt. This seemed to only make the producers more frantic, giving me time-out hand signals and waving me to come off the set.

I felt horrible, but what was more upsetting to me was that my mom was watching and would see that the doll I made for her was a failure. I tried to smile and excused myself from the show for a moment.

"Is something wrong?" I asked the producer at the sideline.

"Are you kidding?" he said, his eyes darting around, looking for something to put on air as quickly as possible.

I started to walk away.

"Marie!" he said. "Every doll we had in stock sold out. You set a QVC collectibles record. Three million dollars in less than fifteen minutes!"

When I got back to my dressing room the head of QVC programming was on the phone. He said, "We had to get you off the air. You were melting down our phone system."

I hung up the phone feeling elated. Breaking a record was great, but I was through the roof feeling like I had gained acceptance as a true doll artist among the collectors. I always knew that I could design dolls, especially from all of my real-life experience working with the best costume designers in the world, as well as hairstylists and makeup artists. But to create a face myself and have people like the resulting doll was, for me, as good as going to number one on the Billboard charts.

In the same way that we emotionally connect to a good song, a doll can take you to a memory, a time of innocence, a life before complications and heartache. I know this is why it was so difficult for me to sculpt myself as a baby. Looking closely for hours at the photo of myself that I was using as a model released in me a mixture of many unexpected feelings.

I wept knowing that I was now parentless. I smiled at the memory of hearing how my father had cried when I was born, so happy he was to finally have a little girl. Recalling the pain of my shyness as a young girl made me feel sorrow. Thinking of my strong faith and values as a teenager gave me a feeling of self-esteem, and, at the same time, regret that my self-esteem was so often injured over the years, drained away by life situations. In this photo of me as a baby I'm willing and trusting, not knowing that disappointment but also unbelievable fortune, heartbreak but also help, hope, and kindness from people who will love me, all lay ahead. Every experience shapes me, changes me, and molds me into who I am today. I thought about the characteristics being molded into my own children from my choices and attitude.

I looked at this picture of me and saw millions of other babies. We do all look quite alike in those first weeks. Like fresh blocks of clay, unmarked but also undefined.

Clay has been used for thousands of years, not just for shaping and creating, but also for its power to absorb the bad (toxins and pollutants) and provide the good (healing and purification). It's adaptable, strong, and can come through the fire. It's perfect for self-portraits.

I refilled the saucer with some clear water, dipped my fingers, and began to shape the clay that would become a doll. Me, as an innocent baby, being sculpted by hands that belonged to the woman I had become. A woman with a bit of knowledge that only comes through time: We've got to get life under our fingernails if we want to create something worth keeping. I'm all for loving ourselves enough to use the good china in the process.

DRESSED TO
SPILL . . . OUT

Talk about pressure on Jonathan (Roberts) and me to perform on Dancing with the Stars! *Not only did my brothers Jimmy, Merrill, and Jay show up to watch, but International Ballroom Champion Shirley Ballas was in the front row. I about fainted. (Not really.)*

Osmond Family Archive

At this point in my career, I can leap to conclusions. When it was taking three adult women to get me dressed, I knew it was time to change course and improvise.

"Suck it in," my girlfriend and coworker tried to say softly as she stood behind me. But the physical exertion from her attempting to zip up my gown turned her whisper into a battle cry.

The other two women in my dressing room trailer were employees of the studio costume department, and they had arrived to help me get dressed. Each one gripped a side of my cherry-red sequined tango dress and pulled toward the center of my back. Those two women would never have been so inappropriate as to tell me to "suck it in," though one's face was sweaty and creased, like a woman in labor, and I think the other was cursing me in Hungarian. They had not known me for twenty-three years, like my girlfriend. She no longer felt the need to mince words with me, and she had no problem mincing my flesh if that's what it would take to get me dressed in time for the show.

"Did you know that the term 'liposuction' was derived from the original Latin phrase 'Suck it in'?" I offered up, a bit of humor to calm the feeling of crisis. I learned that method from my mother.

One of my dressing assistants burst into laughter and then began to weep with equal passion.

"This is never going to work." Her voice trembled in defeat as the stage manager knocked on the trailer door and leaned in momentarily.

"We need you now, Marie," he said. "Eight minutes to air!"

I smiled and answered as if the stage manager were announcing something as casual as the chance to view a gorgeous sunset.

"We've got a little costume malfunction," I said and flailed my hand in the universal "leave us alone" gesture. "I'm really close to being ready. We need to fix one minor problem and I can't move right now. We are hurrying as fast as we can. Be with you in a sec. . . ." I rattled on for about fifteen or twenty secs, buying time. This was yet another worry-pacifying trick I learned from my mom.

The door closed and I heard a voice on the stage manager's walkie-talkie blurting out, "Where is she? This show is live!"

"Push my back fat below my waistline and then zip," I advised, as I gulped in a short breath and tried to relocate my floating ribs into a locked position under my earlobes.

My girlfriend used her knuckles to knead my skin inside the fabric as she micro-moved the zipper upward. There was no place for it all to go anymore. I half expected well-formed French fries to squeeze out near my hip in the same way it does on my son's Play-Doh Happy Meal set.

I wondered if it was the actual French fry I snitched from Abby's plate the previous night that made my costume no longer fit. I had tried this gown on twenty-four hours before and it was too big, needing a whole inch taken in. Randall, the head designer, had congratulated me on my diet discipline. "Three inches!" he announced, noting how much my waistline had lost since the first week of *Dancing with the Stars.*

"That probably explained it," I thought. Randall's assistant assumed he meant for my dress to be taken in three inches. The extreme alteration had turned the under-wires of the bodice into bulldozer shovels and, thanks to the physical inheritance — also from my mother — if I had dropped my chin, I would have suffocated.

I made an executive decision about the dress, partly because we were seven minutes away from an audience of 25 million viewers, but mostly because there was already one Dolly Parton and, as much as I love her, one is enough.

"Forget the zipper!" I said. "Plan B. Ready? Go!"

The other dressing assistant produced her emergency sewing kit, which happened to contain a spool of stretch lace that matched the edging of my dress.

A bees' nest of fast and furious ideas poured out of all four of us on how to fix the problem. Velcro, clear plastic, fish netting, and finally a pullover sweater were offered up.

Since I was the one who had to actually wear the dress onstage, I decide that I would be the "Queen Bee."

"Cool it!" I piped up above the buzzing. "I'm the emergency designer. We need one vision. I've had this happen before . . . when I was pregnant. Do what I say! Please!"

Though my two dressing assistants appeared confused, I didn't have time to explain my past makeshift designs on the *Donny & Marie* talk show when my "with child" body changed so rapidly that wardrobe fittings were useless. The shows where I was never seen rising from my chair were the ones where my blouse had been slit up the back to make room for my belly, and then held in place with duct tape.

The duct tape rescue wouldn't work on this show. I had to dance.

I unrolled the spool of stretch lace onto the counter and each of the three women cut off a long piece. My plan was to fold the zipper under and attach lace across the back to hold the dress in place. I hoped.

The stage manager opened the trailer door again. "Three minutes! And it will take us two minutes to walk to the stage, Marie. The world awaits your arrival."

Stage managers who have a calm presence and the ability to move celebrities around despite chaos are in high demand. This one was a master at his job because he was still smiling, even though the veins on his neck were sticking out far enough to have hung macramé plant holders off of them. He took my hand and helped me down the trailer steps and we walked with the three women clinging to my back, stitching a moving target with a precision that would challenge the skills of the best surgeon.

In the opening moments on *Dancing with the Stars,* host Tom Bergeron announces each couple as they descend one of the long lighted staircases that bookend the orchestra. On the back side of the sparkling set wall is merely a flight of utilitarian aluminum steps rising up to a rugged wood platform behind the glamorous entrance doorway. All of the other celebrities were in their places on the platform, waiting for their names to be called, when I finally made it to the set. Jonathan Roberts, my professional dance partner for the season, sighed in relief when I joined him.

"When we get down to the dance floor," I said to him, "I'm going to stand in front of you. Wrap your arms around my waist and cover my back. Don't let go!"

Jonathan looked confused until he viewed my shoulder blades, with the various pieces of crisscrossed lace, a jaunty zipper seam, and some netting hanging out of my waistline.

I held my shoulders high, clutched my arms to my sides to keep the top half of the dress from drooping, and smiled while we made our show-opening entrance. As timing would have it, our tango wasn't scheduled until the second half of the show, giving my emergency costume sewing crew twenty minutes to put me back together again. It was probably the fastest redesigned gown in television history, and when Jonathan and I took to the floor for our tango, I was saying a silent prayer that all the pieces stayed in place. No Super Bowl Janet Jackson mishaps for me!

Later that evening, one of the dressing assistants arrived to retrieve my dress from my trailer.

"I wanted to thank you," she said, scooping up the costume jewelry bracelets from the countertop.

"No, I have to thank you!" I replied. "The two of you saved my life tonight."

She leaned toward me and dropped her voice. "You were so calm about it, though. Other celebrities on this show would have had a meltdown on us. It was almost fun with you."

I had to hug her. "Listen," I said. "You know I don't drink or do illegal drugs, so I have to get a 'buzz' from somewhere. And there's nothing like the adrenaline rush of a good wardrobe malfunction to make you feel really alive!"

Maybe it's my years of being on the road, or having so many brothers, or so many kids, or having so many more complicated things happen in my life, but I can't imagine having a meltdown over a dress. I hope I never do. And if I do, I think I'll realize that it's time to exit my entertainment career. As my daddy taught me early on when we toured as a family singing group: "It's all for one and one for all." I may be the one in the public eye, but I know I'm the face of a team of people who put their talent, their hearts, and their time into getting me there. A dress will come and go, but the people around you will remember, for years, their interaction with you. And it's people who have the power to bring happiness, never a gown. Not even a gorgeous, sequined, feathered, too-tight gown! Other people lift you up, especially when your dress is held together with lace, pins, and a prayer.

After the dressing assistant left, I looked over at my girlfriend, who was enjoying a piece of crunchy toffee between two slices of breakfast Danish, like a sandwich. She had made one for me, too. As every female knows, after a good rush of adrenaline, you've got to replace your blood sugar.

You'll Be There

On the tour bus with my brother Jimmy and my forever "partner in crime" and true-blue friend since age ten, Patty Leoni. She's the sister I never had.
Osmond Family Archive

The first time I became an aunt I was only ten years old. I loved the idea of being an aunt, and still do, from that first Osmond grandchild, Aaron, through forty-eight more nieces and nephews, all the way to Jimmy's youngest child, sweet little Bella. They all call me "Auntie M," exactly like the character in *The Wizard of Oz* movie. Hey, hold on a minute! Wasn't Auntie Em prematurely gray and a drab dresser who spends her days counting chickens? That does it! Not one of them is invited into my tornado cellar.

My nieces and nephews are charming, smart, amazing people. I know I'm biased, but they truly do represent their parents well in their communities and the world. The adult ones are teachers, nurses, creative entrepreneurs, businesspeople, involved moms and dads, and even entertainers. The ones who are still children really have it together, too! Many of them are honor roll students, involved in team sports, play musical instruments, have been in bands or choirs, and do a lot of volunteer work. My brother Alan's eight sons formed the singing group the Osmonds Second Generation (2ndG), and they do shows throughout the year. Almost all of the young men served two-year missions for our church.

As much as I love every single one of them, one niece in particular really changed my life in a significant and lasting way. She has never called me "Aunt" and I haven't seen her face-to-face in many years, but I think about her often and carry her in my heart. She was born in 1981, at a time when I was just getting ready to forge out on my own and sample a new life, independent of my family.

I had decided I was ready to leave Utah and live in Manhattan and study acting. My parents weren't all too thrilled at the prospect of having me relocate two thousand miles away from them, but they had always encouraged each of us to expand our minds and our talents and couldn't really voice too much opposition to my dream. My best friend, Patty, was ready to make the move with me. I thought I would finally be able to make my own choices without having to always consider how it would affect ten other people. As much as I love my family, I was young and single and saw no reason not to pursue my own goals.

One afternoon, Patty and I were sitting on one of the benches at the extra-large dining table my father had built into the bay window of the kitchen, talking about our future plans. I'm sure, in her highly organized way, she had a steno pad and pen poised.

When the phone rang, I jumped up right away because we were expecting news about the birth of my brother Tom's fifth child. My mother had called earlier to tell me she was at the hospital with him and his wife.

This was before wireless phones, so our rotary-dial wall phone had an extra-long cord on it. In my family it was a top priority to be able to travel from the sink to the stove to the refrigerator without setting the phone down. The cord on this phone was so long you could have roped calves with it. On this day, I stretched the phone cord over to the table so Patty could hear all the good news, too.

Unexpectedly, my mother's voice was filled with sadness. I could feel my heart start to pound under my rib cage. I was afraid to hear what she would say.

"Tommy's baby was born a couple of

minutes ago," she said, her voice cracking with emotion. "It's a girl. But the doctors don't expect her to live long."

I stood, stunned, tugging on the long phone cord, as if the information coming through it was garbled and wrong.

"Your brother is standing next to me and wants to say something to you," my mother told me. Then I could hear Tom on the phone, though due to his hearing impairment I knew he would never be able to hear me.

There were sobs coming from my brother that wrenched my stomach and made my legs feel like they would collapse under me. I had never heard him cry that way. I have always been close to Tom and I knew that he and his wife were struggling in their marriage. At this point, the tragedy of losing a baby seemed to be a heartache that would be unbearable.

"Hello, my only sister," Tom said. "Can you hear me? I need you." That was all he was able to say before handing the phone to our mother.

My mother managed to explain to me that the baby had never developed a skull, leaving her brain massively damaged. It was a miracle that she had survived to full term, let alone the birth.

I had gone numb with shock.

"They named her Jennifer," my mother said. "She's a beautiful baby. You need to come to the hospital right now to see her."

"I can't," I said. "I know I can't see her. I'll fall apart."

Being around sick or injured children had always affected me deeply. I couldn't stop my overwhelming feelings of sorrow that something so awful could happen to a small child. I was terrified to see my tiny helpless newborn niece, to hurt for her. I couldn't face my brother's pain knowing that there would be nothing I could do to fix it.

"Marie, your brother needs you," my mother said softly.

After she hung up, I stood in the middle of the kitchen floor with the phone in my hand, not knowing what to do next. How could I possibly help my brother get through this when it was doubtful I would be able to get through it myself?

Finally, after listening to the dial tone for an endless amount of time, I turned around to hang the phone back into its cradle. As I walked toward the wall some incredibly vivid images flooded my mind as clearly as though they were happening before my eyes. I saw myself in a divine place. I was saying good-bye to people, as if leaving a preexistence, getting ready to join my family. A small girl ran toward me and threw her arms around my waist. I could see her long dark hair and her face tilted up toward mine. And she said: "You'll be there, won't you? You promise?"

This vision only lasted for seconds, but it left me full of purpose. The fear I felt began to melt away. I knew I needed to go directly to the hospital to see that special little spirit before she left behind her mortal body and went back "home."

I told Patty about these strong images and she jumped to her feet and grabbed her purse from the table.

"Get in my car right now, nerd," she said, using the term of affection we've always called one another. "You made a promise to be there. You can't miss this one. Come on, I'm driving."

When we arrived at the hospital, I must admit that I felt a moment of hesitation before I went in. Could I explain to anyone in my family what I had experienced? Would it be of comfort? As I stepped through the door of the private room, I said a prayer that I would be helpful in any way possible. The worry disappeared completely and was replaced with a peace that I have always found when I give the issue over to God. I felt my Father in Heaven was strongly prompting me to be present and willing to listen.

I wrapped my arms around Tom's neck and looked at him, directly, so he could read my lips very clearly. I wanted him to know what I had experienced. He hugged me and cried. Then Tom placed his little daughter in my arms. Her skin was almost ice blue and a tiny medical cap masked the damage to her head. I knew I was there to say good-bye to this sweet infant, but when I held her it didn't feel like a parting to me. It seemed like a "greeting." She was giving me a message, the start of a whole new perspective on life. I put my finger in her tiny hand and she gave it a squeeze accompanied by a tiny smile. When I told those around me that Jennifer had closed her fingers over mine and squeezed, the attending physician told me, "She doesn't know what she's doing. It was just an involuntary reflex."

I looked over at Tom and he smiled at me. I could tell that we were both thinking that this tiny message was not coincidence. She was one little angel who knew exactly what she was here to do. She had reunited us all, once again, and helped us remember that family is most important and eternal. Her short time as an Osmond sparked in me a mission of my own. My desires shifted that day. I was no longer concerned about success in acting class, or life as a single girl, or any of my other self-designed quests. My attention turned away from what I wanted for my own life and toward what was needed by others, mostly those little ones who struggled with illness or injury. She helped me, a fearful person, by giving me the gift of loving to be near and helping as many children as I can with any medical condition: from burns to brain tumors, from arthritis to AIDS. Jennifer was an impetus in the creation of Children's Miracle Network, which, in turn, helps more than 17 million children and their families every single year.

Knowing baby Jennifer, though only for a few hours, led me to a deeper understanding of this "proving ground," as my father called this lifetime. It seems that no matter how many hours, days, and years we are here, our purpose is to eventually return the spirit to "home," to a greater life to come. But in the meantime, it's up to us individually to decide how much we will learn and grow in spirit, even through the weaknesses and strengths of being in a body.

For me, the challenges of bringing both the spirit and the body together toward the same purpose is far less overwhelming when I stay open to what I think of as guiding messages, received from a heavenly source. Having the image of Tom's daughter asking me to "be there" seemed to be one such message that gave me clear guidance. Other times there have been signs in nature that have given me immense comfort.

Following my mother's funeral service in May of 2004 (she had passed away on Mother's Day), family and friends all gathered at the grave site for prayer and a final word. As more than one hundred of us stood together on the cemetery hillside, a pair of monarch butterflies appeared fluttering together over the flowers covering the casket. It was unusually early in the year for butterflies to emerge. In the spring breeze they first danced near the head of my grieving father and then proceeded to fly around each of my brothers and me. As if that wasn't awe-inspiring enough, the pair of monarchs, in unison, found each of my nieces and nephews and my own children in the crowd and momentarily glided near their faces. It did not go unnoticed by many. Even the youngest children began to smile as the butterfly pair circled their heads.

I'm certain you could line up many skeptics who would tell you that this, too, was only a coincidence. I choose to believe otherwise. I think it was a heavenly message from my mother, proof that she was still with us in spirit. A Native American friend of mine confirmed that this was a traditional belief in his culture. As he told me: the butterfly represents the presence of good spirits, peace, beauty, and metamorphosis.

Being the only girl in the family, I was the one who had made certain that everything at my mother's funeral was exactly the way she would have wanted it. Between making all of the arrangements, from the flowers to the program, talking to the press, greeting more than five hundred people who attended the funeral, and at the same time checking in to see that my father, my brothers, and my own children were doing as well as could be expected, I had no time to mourn for my mom. I had to return to doing my five-hour-a-day radio show on the following Monday, and prepare for the next QVC show as well. The pace of life caught me up full-time, and I just pressed on without stopping to reflect and grieve.

The following year, on Mother's Day, I found myself almost unable to function; I was missing my mom so deeply. I knew I needed to take a couple of hours alone, to give myself time to mourn losing her. After calling in a babysitter, I got into my car to drive up into the mountains.

The mountains are the one place I go to truly find peace and refuel my spirit. To sit in an aspen grove, or on a rock overhang, or near running water gives me an almost instant sense of emotional recovery. I guess if you want to truly feel grounded, go outside and put yourself down on the ground! Whenever my children are anxious or hyper, we go to a park and lie on the grass and take in the sky above us.

About five miles out of town, I had an image totally contrary to my initial thought of finding some peace at high altitudes. I saw myself at the mall in one of my favorite department stores.

I tried to shake the thought from my head, but it was persistent.

"Oh, please!" I said to myself out loud. "You only want to shop to anesthetize the pain. Not a good idea." I tried to shrug it off. I pressed down on the gas pedal, but it took concentrated force to make my foot react. Every impulse in my body was to turn the car around and head to the mall.

Shopping was something that my mother and I did together if we needed to cheer up a bit. We'd sneak away for an hour or two and buy some inexpensive or fun thing that made us smile. Then we would find an ice-cream parlor and splurge on sundaes, promising not to tell anyone that we had.

The memory made my heart ache with loneliness for her.

"Marie, you are so dysfunctional," I said out loud to myself. "Shopping is not the answer." I put on my sunglasses and started to cry.

Again, I felt a strong urge to turn the car around and head to the mall. This time, before my logical reasoning got in the way, my body stopped the car, made a U-turn, and headed back down the mountain.

When I entered the department store, I stopped inside of the door. "Okay. Fine. Where to?" I thought.

I felt prompted to take the escalator up one floor to a section of the store I had never shopped in before. I started to giggle; I had no idea why I felt compelled to go to that particular area, as it seemed like the "grandma" section, not trendy or even what I would consider fun clothing.

When the clerk asked if she could help me, I wanted to say: "Do you have any idea why I'm here?" But I thought she might think I needed a different kind of help, so I casually said I was "just looking."

I started to leave the area, feeling embarrassed, when a thought hit me strongly.

Turn around!

I searched only for a moment before one tiny bit of fabric protruding from a rack of skirts caught my eye. It was a colorful butterfly against a black background. I moved the other clothes aside to see the full skirt. It was covered with hundreds of multicolored butterflies, from the waistband to the hem. There was only one like it on the rack and it was exactly my size. It seems my mother had taken me shopping again, and, in the fastest way possible, had assured me that she was still there with me.

My mother always had a silent way to show her feelings to each of her children. She would take us by the hand and squeeze it three times to represent the words "I love you." In the last months of my mother's life, when she was unable to speak, she continued to squeeze my hand three times every day as I sat by her bedside. Both she and baby Jennifer, unable to use words, had sent me a message through a tiny squeeze. Though both are physically gone, they continue to gently squeeze my spirit, to open my eyes to the guidance and help that are available to me if I am open, and in turn, to ways that I can guide and help others.

I bought the butterfly skirt. I knew my mom would want me to have it. To assure my mother that I had heard her message very clearly, I took that skirt out for an ice-cream sundae on the way home.

ACKNOWLEDGMENTS

Tons of gratitude to all who generously offered their time, talents, and care to this book:

Those who put me on track:
John Ferriter, my William Morris agent . . . your enthusiasm has never wavered. I love you.
Mel Berger at William Morris Agency . . . thanks for believing in me.
Tracy Bernstein at New American Library.
Marleah Leslie and Ann Gurrola, my publicists.
And those who keep me on track:
My fans . . . whose amazing loyalty keeps me moving forward.
For reading pages with insightful editing eyes, listening to stories, and sharing profound perspectives and helpful ideas: Teresa Fischer, Patricia Bechdolt, Patty Leoni, Michelle Osmond, Connie Ljunberg, Darla

and Greg Sperry, Gail Ryan, Lorraine Wheeler, Cheryl Burke and her Tai Pan crew.

For assistance with the photographs and for being patient about looking at my mug over and over and over and over again: Peggy Vicioso, Tina Salmon, Debra Mac-Farlane, Kirsten Gallo, Debra Gehris, Toni Sorenson, Cashman Photography, Stacie Mullen of NutriSystem, and Megan Lozito and Leslie Holland of the American Heart Association.

And finally, those who keep me from derailing:

Kim
Photo by: Kim Goodwin

Kim Goodwin (my Kimmy, what a talent: makeup, hairstylist, photography, designer):

370

For being the miracle who reappears in my life exactly when I need you most. Whether you like it or not, you are now part of my family.

Jimmy
Osmond Family Archive

To my brother, Jimmy Osmond. You are the life raft in every storm. I don't know what I would do without you, and I would do anything for you.

Karl

Osmond Family Archive

My continued love and gratitude to my manager, Karl Engemann, aka the God-father, the Grand Poobah, the Silver Fox, or often referred to as the Human Q-tip. In a sense you've raised me and, through your wisdom, guided me through decades of decisions, choices, and challenges with your incredibly gentle heart that has remained my one true constant through it all. I love you.

Marcia

Photo by: Kim Goodwin

Special thanks to my coauthor, Marcia Wilkie. I'll never forget when we met ten years ago as you burst into my dressing room in Filene's Basement!!!! . . . okay . . . it was backstage . . . with your "head writer" steno pad and a mischievous grin. I knew we'd work (and play) together for years to come. How's that for good intuition??? You are one of the most talented women I've ever known. We're the perfect blend of third-grade humor, intellectual curiosity, and spiritual awe. Most important, I know we're friends till the end. By the way . . . did you change your cell phone number?

My endless devotion to the eight people I

love more than any words can express, my children: Stephen, Jessica, Rachael, Michael, Brandon, Brianna, Matthew, and Abigail. You are my source of daily love, joy, "aha" moments, tears, inspiration, and some pretty hefty laughter. You give me so many things to ponder on . . . and some to even write about. You are my world!

And always, eternal gratitude to my loving Father in Heaven, who gives purpose to everything.

ABOUT THE AUTHOR

Marie Osmond endeared herself to an entire generation as the star of numerous award-winning television shows and specials, as a multimillion-selling recording artist, and as a worldwide concert-tour headliner. She is also a *New York Times* bestselling author, has appeared on Broadway, and is the entrepreneur behind the successful Marie Osmond Collector Dolls. She is the mother of eight beautiful children, which she considers her greatest achievement.

The employees of Thorndike Press hope you have enjoyed this Large Print book. All our Thorndike, Wheeler, and Kennebec Large Print titles are designed for easy reading, and all our books are made to last. Other Thorndike Press Large Print books are available at your library, through selected bookstores, or directly from us.

For information about titles, please call:
   (800) 223-1244

or visit our Web site at:
   http://gale.cengage.com/thorndike

To share your comments, please write:
   Publisher
   Thorndike Press
   295 Kennedy Memorial Drive
   Waterville, ME 04901